THE BOOK ON SALES

How to Earn the Business

Ronnie Andrews

10-10-10
Publishing

THE BOOK ON SALES/EARN THE BUSINESS
www.businessearned.com

Copyright © 2020 RONNIE ANDREWS

ISBN: 978-1-77277-328-6

Limits of Liability and Disclaimer of Warranty
The author and publisher shall not be liable for your misuse of the enclosed material. This book is strictly for informational and educational purposes only.

Warning - Disclaimer
The purpose of this book is to educate and entertain. The author and/or publisher do not guarantee that anyone following these techniques, suggestions, tips, ideas, or strategies will become successful. The author and/or publisher shall have neither liability nor responsibility to anyone with respect to any loss or damage caused, or alleged to be caused, directly or indirectly by the information contained in this book.

Publisher
10-10-10 Publishing
Markham, ON Canada

Printed in Canada and the United States of America

Table of Contents

Foreword

Do you know your purpose in life? If you are like most people, you probably don't. You may find yourself running harder and still falling short of your goals and the life you dream of. But regardless of what you may think about yourself, know that you have greatness inside of you. And if you are interested in sales, this is the book for you!

Author Ronnie Andrews is a very successful salesperson with 37 years of experience, and he has discovered some powerful secrets on how to have a successful professional sales career.

As you follow his powerful system you will begin to achieve measurable successes, month by month. As you track your successes, you will begin to move even closer to fully creating, and then living, the life you are dreaming of.

This book will be your companion every step of the way. Take ownership of your life and future, rather than sitting back and simply letting life happen to you. Take charge, and accept full responsibility for everything in your life. Begin today, to create the life that you want. There is no greater accomplishment than moving forward and starting to live the life of your highest vision.

I wish you great success on your journey.

Raymond Aaron
New York Times Bestselling Author

Acknowledgements

I would like to thank my Lord and Savior Jesus Christ. My wife Deanise Andrews who has stuck with me through the hard times (thank you). Thanks to my mother and father B.J. and Evelyn Andrews for showing me how to build a strong foundation in life. Thanks to my kids Demarco Ronshon Andrews and his wife Michele Harris-Andrews, Demetris Andrews, and Edna Andrews Fisher. I call my kids my research and development team. If I need to find something or research anything, they are the best at getting the job done.

I want to give thanks to my siblings John and Emma Andrews (wife), Marie Andrews Bonner, Edna and Frank Forney (husband), Wilson and Gerdine Andrews (wife), Barbara Andrews Warren, Betty Jackson and my 2 deceased brothers B.J. Andrews Jr. and James Andrews. You guys have a major impact on the foundation of my life. Thank you!

I want to acknowledge and thank my brother from another mother, Sandy Billings. I talk to Sandy 3 to 4 times a week. It's our power talk where we talk about business, money, motivation, and investments. If you don't have someone that you can have a power talk with weekly, then you are missing out because it really keeps you focused.

Major thanks to my church family, my Senior Pastor Dr.Creflo and Pastor Taffi Dollar. My local Pastors Horace and Pastor Yvonne Holmes. The vision keepers Travis Harrell, Willie Smith, Edward Risper, Kelnard Murray, Daryl Clark, Darrell Banks, Deloris Bentley, Diane Coady, Edward Lewis, Bill and Marilyn Lewis.

I had the wonderful opportunity to work for an Automotive Company (WH) that I want to thank as well. I learned a lot from them because they were very organized, disciplined and productive. I had the pleasure to work for an Insurance Company (PFS) whom also had a great impact on my life and success. I'm forever grateful and thankful for them too. I worked in a factory for 18 years, Rheem MFC. I met so many good people; I can't recall all of the names, but thank you my Rheem family.

To the soldiers I served with and all the soldiers out there, thank you for your service.

One last major shout-out to Baldwin High Class of 1976. You all have major impact on my life. I love you all!!!

I hope I didn't miss anyone but to every company and everyone mentioned, again thank you so much for being a powerful source in my life.

Chapter 1

The Fundamentals of Sales

The Training (Train Yourself)

Do you remember when you got hired by a sales company? I do—they would train you for a month, maybe three months, but those days are gone. In today's business world, you have to train yourself. Now they have a training period just to say you had training. It's not training—trust me—and this is why there is a high turnover in sales. So buy the books, get the CDs, and do what you have to do in order to win.

This book is about getting you prepared to take on any sales position—the fundamentals and step-by-step guide to having a successful professional career in sales. Just to tell you a little about myself, and to show you the mistakes that I've made, and how to learn from them, I joined the army right out of high school because I needed the money for college. I knew a college degree would be possible in the Army. The first year, I had to get used to the army life. My last two years of college, I chose to major in business correspondence. So, two things happened: I got a college degree, and I served my country proudly. When I returned home to get a degree in business correspondence from Georgia Military College (also known as GMC), it was only paying minimum wage. So I changed my major to business, which is a step above business correspondence. As I started over, I used some of the information from my business correspondence courses to go towards the business degree. After two years of college while in the Army, and two years of GMC, with only two and a half years of credits, things started getting hard with the birth of my first child. Fatherhood caused me to enter the work force; work and college became my life.

This was when I was introduced to sales. Don't get me wrong; I am not against college— college is good—but in my situation, I had to make some decisions. I skipped the next quarter of college to sell insurance part-time. It was tough at times, but I noticed that you could set your own income, if you worked hard at it, got better, did your own training, and built your own training library. I worked in a factory for 18 years, and for 15 out of those 18 years, I sold insurance part-time. I was making more income part-time than at my full-time job. So, I was talking about leaving this job. Everybody was calling me crazy, and saying that it was the highest paying job in the country. It was a good paying job, and people were trying to get in, not leave. So, there I was, with everyone thinking that I was crazy, and I was starting to feel the pressure of not leaving. I will never forget what a certain lady told me. She said, "Ronnie, why don't you stop dreaming? You are not going anywhere; I know I am not." Wow...that hit me hard. That lady did not know anything about me, so how could she say something like that? Like the old saying, that was the straw that broke the camel's back. Well, I started to doubt myself for about two months, and I was thinking, "Maybe she is right; why don't I just make the best of this job?" I brought my books to work, studied on my breaks, and listened to my motivational tapes every chance I could. One guy told me, "You don't need that stuff for this job; you are just wasting your time." WOW!

All of this negative talk got to me. BUT YOU KNOW WHAT? That strong spirit on the inside of me said, "Don't stop dreaming!" You know, life will give you whatever you accept. I am not accepting any more negativity—I don't want to hear it. I left the factory in 1998 and never looked back. There is not, and there will never be, a device that can measure the size of a man's or woman's heart. You have to go and get it; no one is going to bring it to you. Fight hard for what you want— you can do it.

Be Neat and Clean

Have you ever sat in a barber's, beautician's, or salesman's office, and they had bad breath? Well, you don't have to answer that question. You know, being an entrepreneur, you need every edge. There was an Olympic gold medalist runner that once said, "A half a second can cost any runner millions of dollars. When you leave home to do a business transaction— buying real estate, cars insurance, or whatever—you know you want to deal with a professional. If someone greets me with their pants sagging and their clothing not neat, they have already lost the sale. I went to the barber shop one day, and it was my first time being there. The barber was clean and had everything laid out on his table, lined up to the T, in his area, and I said, "That's the guy that will cut my hair; yes sir, he is the man." That guy gave me the worst hair cut I ever had to date. You see, he was not the best, but he looked like the best, giving him the sales. To look good and be good is what this book is about—we are always chasing after excellence. I have talked to a lot of managers that work in the human relations department, who do all of the hiring. Every one of them told me that within the first 15 seconds of meeting a person, they knew whether they would hire the person or not. The first 15 seconds—do you hear me? So that lets you know how important your appearance is.

So when you are on a sales mission, everything counts; you need every edge, every time. Whatever sales profession you choose, dress accordingly. In the old days, if you had facial hair, it would cost you money. In today's business, that doesn't bother a customer, as long as it is trim and neat. You don't want to be too flashy. Make sure your shoes are shining and your clothing is clean and neat. You don't have to spend a lot of money to look good. Just know what looks good on you. I saw a 350-pound person wearing tights—it did not look good at all, but there are some things that I have seen a 350-pound person wear that look good on them. Know what looks good on you, and dress accordingly.

You know, I believe everybody wants to be somebody. No matter who we are or where we come from, deep down, all of us believe that we are special. When we were young, playing sports, we always wanted to be the star, the quarterback, or the doctor. Don't let anyone kill your dreams. Did you ever wonder why people lose the dreams of their childhood—dreams like becoming famous, or living in a fine home, or owning their own business or making lots of money. I believe this is the perfect time for you to make a decision to change your life. You can take advantage of the dream of opportunity that this country was built on. I know there are obstacles out there—overcome them, be tough mentally and physically, and go get it. Sales or marketing may not be your niche. Whatever area you work in to achieve your dreams, finding an environment that encourages you to dream can make a big difference. So, wherever you are (I talk about finding your spot in later chapters), put your all into it—make it happen!

Learn the Language

It doesn't matter what business you are in; there is a certain type of communication (learn the *lingo*, as we call it). You need to know about your business. When I first got into the insurance business, there were words such as *rated, concealment*...I could go on. In the automobile business, there were other words, such as *spot, d-horse*...I could go on in each sales professional business, but I think you get it. The way I look at a professional sales career is like a trade. If you are good, you can go anywhere and sell (check out the chapter on finding your spot). One thing about this trade is that you will need to train yourself every day. You will need to motivate yourself every day. Listen to trainers on CDs every day. To be good, put your work in every day. Learn word tracks, and learn how to overcome objections. Learn the tie-down questions (if you could, would you...?). I will talk about this more in my workshops. Whatever product you sell, learn all about it, inside and out—be the expert. When it comes to selling, I will put myself up against anyone; it does not matter what part of the world they are from. You see, I have put in the work; I have put in the training. When you do what you are supposed to, over the years, you will have that confidence. However, you may just be getting started. This book is for you, and if you use these principles, you will get to where you need to be.

Warning: There is no free lunch—opportunity is missed by most people because it is dressed in overalls and looks like work. You beat 50% of people in America by working hard. You beat another 40% by being a person of honesty and integrity, and by standing for something. The last 10% is a dogfight in the free enterprise system. This is your professional career, so take it seriously—your family is depending on you. Value your customers in any business you are in.

Building value is building your net worth. People are your product, not the product you sell. I remember, back in the 80s, a car company that was doing badly. The quality was at an all-time low. This was iconic: They hired this guy, and he was saying that he was going to do this and that, and on and on. He sold himself—he got the people's minds off bad quality, and on the fact that he would fix everything.   Guess what? The people bought in, and he turned the situation around. His name was Lee Iacocca. When he came to that company, most people had never heard of him. I know I did not. He knew he had what it took to turn a company around. That guy was humiliated and fired from another big iconic car company. He wanted to give up, but he did not.

This is what you have to do: Train yourself every day to be the best, read books, and take an hour every day to do these things. Here is another thing that's very important. When you are getting your day started, start with prayer and meditation. This is just my suggestion. Believe in a power greater than you. I believe in Jesus, but I cannot tell you what to believe in. You have to be ready when the opportunity comes: It is better to be prepared and have no opportunity, than to have opportunity and not be prepared. So, let's sum this up: Here is a guy who worked for a company for 38 years, and for 8 of those years, he was the top executive (pure royalty) and had everything, including the big office suite (you get the idea). He got fired, lost it all, and was hired by a sinking company that was about to go out of business. That could have been the end of the story, but GUESS what? It did not end there. He got that company back making money, with better products and better customer relations, and every good thing to get the company back on top again—and he was back on top too.

What I'm telling you is that you should never give up—don't ever give up. This book is about people themselves, not the blue bloods, those who got their money the old-fashioned way (by inheriting it), and about the common and not so common. It's about people who were programmed to believe that average was the best they could hope for. Never stop dreaming. Quitting is easy; anybody can quit—in fact, most people do. You have what it takes, and I will make sure you win.

Be Articulate

Now, this can be a hard one. *Articulate* means having or showing the ability to speak fluently and coherently, or expressing a feeling or an idea fluently or coherently. Let me break it down for you. Have you ever given a speech or presentation, and when it was over, you said to yourself that it was lousy. You knew that you had done a bad job, and it made you feel horrible. I have been there, and I made up in my mind that it would not happen again. The opposite of that would be, when you finish the presentation, you would say to yourself that you knocked it out the park. There are two different endings, and I know which one is best. This book will train you in those areas. What makes the difference? We will dive deep and let you know. Are you willing to do the work? Let's get busy. You will hear me repeat some things a few times, and that is because it's important. You can't be ordinary and average; you have to do what other people want to do, and that is to work at it harder. When you find your spot (you may already be there, and I will talk more about finding your spot, later on in this book), learn your product. Create a presentation that fits your style. Some companies have their own presentation in place. Learn it and get good at it. Getting good is the next level of income for you and your family. If you do this, you would stand out from your peers. Use your cell phone to record yourself, listen to it, and do it over and over. The idea is to get it down so well that when you have a customer in front of you, you want to wow them. You are the expert and the professional, and the customer will see that you are, and will tell others to see you. When I joined the Army, we trained and trained in the same things, over and over. I got so tired of doing the same thing that it nearly made me sick; but when that time came—and it did— my training (mind) automatically took control instantly, and dealt with the situation, and it saved my life. This is why you have to drill this into yourself—because it works. You will know how to overcome any objections, and be prepared for anything. When you put the work in on yourself every day, you put the power of the universe to work for you. Wow, it's like the more you put it in, the more it comes out to you. Life can't be cheated; you have to go after it—you own the right to claim it. Let me tell you the good news: You don't have to take whatever situation you are in; you don't have to continue your life that way; you don't have to be average and ordinary; you don't have to let people put you down.

You have to get back that childlike ability to dream again. You have to start believing again that you are special. You have to see yourself winning again. You have to see yourself doing something special with your life, being somebody, being different again. Keep dreaming, and I will see you at the top!

Cold Calls

"Cold calls" might be seen as being a little out of place, but I put it here because there is a lot to gain doing cold calls. I hated cold calls at first, for a long time. Over the years, doing cold calls helped me so much, but I could not tell at the time. Looking back now, it is one of the best ingredients of becoming a professional salesperson. You see, your goal is to not have to cold call as you grow in your profession. If you have to, you will not be afraid, but you might have to from time to time. When I had to first cold call, man, I was scared. As I kept doing it, cold calls helped me to not be scared anymore. Whatever you fear the most, you should do the most. I never forgot the day when I got the phone book and just started calling people. I would say, "This is Ronnie Andrews from ABC Company. I see that we have an appointment with you on Friday. Do you have any questions before you come in? I got a lot of hanging up in my face. Some people let me know that I had the wrong person. Lonesome, older people would be glad you called so that they had someone to talk to. And some people would say that it must be God, because they did not have an appointment with you, but they needed your service...Bang! I had to go through a lot of people to get that one, but it pays. It builds your confidence when you train yourself this way.

The more you do it, the more you don't fear anything when it comes to a customer. Don't get me wrong; some of those people cursed me out. I would just apologize: "Sir, I am sorry," or "Ma'am, it was my mistake," and on and on. You would not believe the confidence this will give you. Cold calling helps with speeches and presentations. You see, the more I practiced with one company, and when they had a problem with a tough customer, they would ask me to call them, because I was good at handling any situation. I had to make 550 to 700 calls a month to get 65 appointments and 21 sales for the month. It's all about the numbers when it comes to professional sales. So, you should learn how to get comfortable on the phone and in person. I talk about getting comfortable, in a later chapter. As a professional salesperson, you have to put your month together like a puzzle. I had the opportunity to operate in three different sales industries: insurance, automobile, and my own t-shirt business. I will use the automobile industry to show you how to put a month together. When a month starts, you should call the customers in your database. You don't have to cold call at this time. You only cold call when you run out of people to call or you just want to practice your skills. You are calling your appointments, the ones that said to get back to them. You also want to call the ones that get to their two mark; that is about the time they start thinking about a new vehicle. You will have the customer with total loss in an accident. You have people calling in asking about vehicles; you also have customers coming to your place of business. Then you have your referral sources, people sending you customers, and you have the internet...Wow! Let's sum this up: your database, your 24-month customers, total loss customers, the call-in customers, the walk-in customers, your referral sources, and the internet. People use these tips, and it will double or triple your income.

Remember that cold calls are good for your professional growth—do it as much as you can. So many people feel like their lives belong to somebody else. They feel like they've lost control, like they are puppets, and somebody else is pulling the strings. Wrong! Get rid of that belief so that you will succeed!!! Pull YOUR OWN STRINGS!!!

The Sports Theory of Fundamentals

I hope you noticed the name of this chapter, and if you played any sports, you know how important fundamentals are. I love all sports, but I was best at baseball; and in baseball, your coach will tell you to watch the ball to the bat when you are hitting. When you are catching the ball, watch the ball into the glove. The basic stuff, right? Well, that is the way professional sales are—you have to build your career with the small, simple things first. Make the phone calls, do your follow-up, and keep a log—most companies have a database to put your customer's information in (log it). Building your career should be important to you. You can have great financial success in the profession, but you have to put the work in. I have sold in the insurance, automotive, and clothing industries. Customers want the same thing: a good product, a good price, and to be treated well—simple, right?

Let me tell you a story. A friend of mine had an accident in a vehicle that I had sold her, and it was about 8 years old. Most of my customers call me for all car buying situations (the car was totaled out). So, I sent her to a friend because I did not have what she wanted. She bought a car from the friend I had sent her to. She was happy, only to find out 1 day later that the driver's side floor mat had a hole in it. A paper mat had been over it, and she did not see it during the transaction. Now she thinks that the salesperson knew it was there. I don't think he did, but now she said that she will never buy a vehicle from that dealership again. The dealership is a good dealership, and the salesperson is not a bad salesperson; but to her, that is what she sees. She called the salesperson, and he said he would call her back, but he didn't. Maybe he got busy, but no matter what, he should have made sure to call her back. She and her family have bought 5 cars from that dealership. Now she says that she will never buy a car from that place again.

A floor mat might not mean anything to you or me, but to her, it was big. The salesperson should have taken care of it himself. You see, it's the small things that can cost you a big price. Take care of customers, because your customers will take care of you. In professional sales, you will face situations like this often, so just do the right thing—it's not hard.

Train yourself—buy your own books/CDs; go on YouTube—and get training all the time. I have been in sales for over 30 years, but I still buy books and CDs, and go on YouTube. I can't get enough, and you will love it. It can increase your income; in fundamentals, it's the small things that make your career great. I tell all my customers that they can call me anytime. I want them to know that I am with them and for them. They are spending money with you, a lot of it in most cases. Give them the comfort of knowing that they can count on you. When you get their trust, don't lose it. The fundamentals are the foundation on which some things are built upon (to put it in layman's terms); and for us, it is a professional sales career we are building. So build it right; you can't fool people and think they are going to send you prospects. If you do them wrong, they will tell everyone they know.

Chapter 2

Get Comfortable

Body Language

Let me tell you about body language. Body language is the process of communicating non-verbally through conscious and unconscious gestures and movements. WOW! So you can be talking to a prospective client, saying one thing, but your body language could be saying something else. This is something you have to learn how to control, and I will show you how. This also goes back to practicing in the mirror, doing your presentation, so that you can master this part of being a professional salesperson. I knew some salespeople, and when they came to work, you could tell that something was not right at their home. You can't be that way. I also knew some salespeople that were having war at home, but you could not tell. It doesn't matter what goes on in your personal life; you cannot let it spill over into your career.

You can have so much on your mind when you come to your location (your spot). I don't like to say *work,* because if you like what you do, it's not work. When I would get to my spot, I would have an imaginary trash can by the door to put all of my negative junk in before I would go in. When I go in, in the morning, I'm ready. I have had my prayer time and my motivational time, and my head is clear. I see salespeople rubbing their hair, rubbing their beard, and grabbing their noses when they are in front of a customer. When you are in front of a prospect, you have to learn to be professional in all ways. I remember, early in my sales career, when a customer came to my place of business. I greeted them with my usual greeting, I thought. The guy said to me, "Did you have a bad night?" In my mind, I was thinking that I had smiled while doing my usual thing, but the customer showed me that I had not. These are the things you have to be aware of. Body language is so easy to overlook because you don't know you are doing it. Just work on it over and over again. I have seen salespeople walk right by a customer and not see them at all because they have too much on their minds. These are the things you are not aware of, so this is why I am letting you know that they're there. Record yourself using your phone, and you will see things you didn't know that you do.

The overall goals of a professional salesperson are to increase your confidence, professionalism, and ability to deal effectively with any sales situation. A salesperson gains respect through honest, clear, and direct self-expression. When you communicate in an honest, direct manner, customers soon learn to trust you. So just work on these bad habits—trust me, they are there—and the better you get, the higher your income goes. When I was with one of the insurance companies, they had a five-day tough training on this body language. You would have to role play with one of your peers, have a candid speech that you would go by, and you were graded. If you failed, you would do it again until you passed. So, if you have people that you can role play with, do it over and over again. Body language is a big part, but you will get it. The things I put in this book are things I've learned the hard way. I have done the door-to-door and cold calls, and I have made some mistakes. I want you to learn from my mistakes so that you can be on the fast track to success.

Life will turn out the way you see it turning out. You have to start seeing happiness, success, and fulfillment in your life. You have to demand happiness and success for yourself. Make your mind up, put your heart into it, and go for it!

Think

Here is another small word with a large impact. In the sales profession, that means that after listening to the customer talk, you should think before you answer. Be careful not to overthink and not listen to what the customer is saying. It's not hard to do. When you get sincere in what you are doing, it will come easy. The customer will tell you just how to earn their business. The definition of *think* is to "have a particular option, belief, or idea about someone or something." It's our job to find out what it is the customer is wanting to do. How do we do that by listening? Always take two seconds, after a customer finishes talking, before you say anything. That seems to make the customer think that you are listening; and in most cases, you are listening. Have you ever went to a gathering and noticed that everyone was talking as though they knew everything, and you say to yourself, "Do I do that?" Yes, you do. Try it sometimes—it's fun—and you will notice a lots of things that you would not normally notice (at your next gathering, just listen and think). One person wrote a book called *Think and Grow Rich*; so you see, thinking has a lot to do with your success. I guess you have noticed by now that the first five chapters of this book are just fundamentals—building the foundation. The foundation is so important; it's like building a house. Have confidence in yourself; if you do this, you will have great success. This is the way you need to think; there is no alternative to success—it's win or nothing. I want to impress on you that the bad times are over. If any of you think it can't be done, let me tell you that it can and will be done, beyond any possibility of doubt. You have greatness in you. The enemy knows that you have greatness but doesn't want you to discover it; but he is too late—go and be great.

In the first chapter, I talked about cold calling, when you are on the phone. Remember the "think" concept; it's very powerful, and it will help you in every situation. These concepts will make you stand out from the crowd. Most professional salespeople don't go the extra mile. When you go the extra mile, there are only a few there with you.

The customer will know, and the community will know. Everyone you do business with will tell someone how great you are, and will send you business. Get these fundamentals down, and you will be surprised how the business just comes your way. In a later chapter, we will be getting down to the nuts and bolts of sales, so stay tuned.

Here is a power principle that I have for you: You have to demand happiness and success for yourself. The world is not going to give you anything. Nobody is going to come along and hand you an opportunity. That does not mean that you don't have a chance. You have the power to make your own opportunity. All you need is the belief that you deserve a place in the world, and the determination to get it. You can do it, and I am going to help you.

Speak Effectively

We have talked about the training, being neat, learning the language, and so on. Now that we have heard the customer, it's time for the customer to hear us. When it's time for you to speak, please be precise. It's your time to let the customer know why your service will be the best for their situation. Speak clear, and give them a scenario fitting for the situation. By now, you should have your presentation down to the "T" and be able to wow the customer. In your speech, as you talk to the customer, they know that you are a professional and will want to do business with you. If you did the work in the mirror, recording yourself, and all that we talked about earlier, when you get a customer in front of you, it's *show time*. You see, when you do all the fundamentals of training, you will have so much confidence, and you will know that you got the business. That is the way it works.

When you put the time in, no one can deny you. It's a universal law— the more you put in, the more you get out. This is why, when I put my work in, I look for a harvest. Remember the guy I talked about in the previous chapter, who worked for a car company for 38 years? Back in those days, after 38 years of being the top executive at a car company, you could retire quite nicely, but something just didn't feel right to him. He didn't think he was treated right, so he had something to prove—maybe to himself or maybe to the ones who fired him. I don't know, but I do know that he went to a sinking car company after he was let go by that car company, and he turned it around. You have to have determination; you have to dig deep sometimes and go for it. All I'm saying is that you have to believe in yourself. I like this old football coach quote: "The price of success is hard work, dedication to the job at hand, and the determination that, whether we win or lose, we have applied the best of ourselves to the task at hand." In other words, when you have done your best, and you know you have put everything on the line, you win.

Power Principle: You have to learn to dream again.

Stop telling yourself what you can't do, and start thinking about what you really want from life. Let your mind open up to the possibilities, like you did in high school. Believe in yourself. Two-thirds of the battle is in your mind. It's true; belief in yourself is power. Let me tell you about this guy in U.S. history: In 1831, he failed in business; in 1832, he was defeated for legislature; in 1833, he had his second failure in business; in 1836, he suffered a nervous breakdown; in 1838, he was defeated for speaker; in 1840, he was defeated for elector; in 1843, he was defeated for congress; in 1848, he was defeated for congress again; in 1855, he was defeated for senate; in 1856, he was defeated for vice president; in 1858, he was defeated for senate; in 1860, he was elected President of the United States—who was this? Abraham Lincoln. He never stopped competing, even with a pattern of failures. Just keep competing until you win!

Respond Honestly

When dealing with a problem for a customer, be honest. I have seen so many salespeople that will tell a customer anything for that moment. If there is something you don't know, tell them you don't know and that you will find out and get back to them. Being honest is not asking for much. Sometimes telling the truth is not going to sound good to the customer, but when it's all over, the customer will thank you for telling the truth. Being thankful with the customer goes a long way. Treat every customer with royalty. One of the biggest mistakes that salespeople make is to qualify a buyer. I remember one time when a salesperson passed up an opportunity on this one young guy. He just said that he couldn't do anything, and he let the rookie have him. The young guy's mother owned two restaurants. She came in, put the money up front that was needed, and her son left in the vehicle. The rookie salesperson made a $1600 commission. Treat them like they can buy anything in your showroom or in your listing. Never ask a customer if they can afford your product. I can't say this enough: Treat them like millionaires, and they will buy like they have millions. As a salesperson, don't be concerned with whether or not a potential customer is wasting your time. Would you rather blow them off and waste time yourself?

Completely walk through the whole scenario. It is better to spend time with a customer who might be able to buy, than with yourself who for sure is not going to buy. Salespeople do this every day, and though they think otherwise, it does not create the life they want. They worry about people's budgets, ideas, expectations, etc., rather than just treating people incredibly well and then letting them change their own mind, because people can and will change their minds. They will spend more than budgeted, spend money they don't have, and do things they swore they wouldn't do. Selling requires trust, not commitment; selling requires great attitudes, salesmanship, and very little from your buyer. You don't need someone's budget to sell them something. You need a product, a buyer, and excitement.

When you start to belittle a customer, that is the time that they start losing trust in you. Please, customers know when you are telling them a lie, so don't get caught up. Lots of times, when a salesperson lies, the customer knows it as soon as it comes out of their mouth. They might do business with you but will not recommend anyone to you, and will tell people not to use you. Selling is about communication. Salespeople are the greatest communicators, using the purest form of communication. Unlike artists, actors, painters, and singers, the salesperson has no canvas, no script, no stage, no lights, or music—they only have direct communication, with nothing to create the scene but words and gestures from one person to another person. Any mistake in the communication will show up like the wrong paint or the wrong note. Selling is also about life. If you can communicate well, and you have the mindset, then you will get what you want in life; and if you can't, then you will not get what you want. Everyone is a salesperson: The politician is trying to sell you on voting for them; the teacher is trying to get kids to learn; the parent is trying to sell the kids on behaving a certain way—I can go on and on, but you get the picture. Everyone is trying to convince someone of something. It's simple: Treat the customer as though they could do anything. Treat them like royalty, be positive, and don't worry about budgets, payments, payoff, or their momentary expectations. You have seen people who will find the money or find the solution to make it happen. Do you remember the song, "Got to Be Real?" That is how you earn the business.

Remember, You Work for Them!

Have you ever went to a place of business to make a purchase, and a hot-shot salesperson greets you like it's all about him? Some of these people act like you came to be entertained by them—don't forget who you are working for. That being said, find out how you can really help them. Let them know that you are there to serve. One way I like to look at it is to make your professional career a crusade. Let me give you a few examples. When I first got into the insurance industry, I studied the industry and every type of policy that was out there. I did that because I knew that there were some bad ones out there. When I got myself ready, I could go into any home, tell them to go get their policy, and if it was a bad one, I would destroy it. Sometimes the customer would call me after I had left their home, and after they had talked to their old agent. They would want me to show them in front of the old agent. I have set up many of these meetings with customers and their old agents—only one has shown up, and I recruited him and he came to work for us. You have to be a student of your profession. Whatever career you're in, you have to go the extra mile and study it. A crusade adds meaning and purpose to your life. You see, I didn't destroy those insurance policies to show up the other agent. I wanted to show them that I cared, and the truth, even if they didn't do business with me (most of them did go with my product). When I got into the automobile industry, I did the same things—I studied the industry, the product, and the competitors. Before I would sell a vehicle, I would do a product knowledge demonstration (show time) to earn the business, and I would get serious. Sometimes the customer would say that they did not know that the vehicle did that, and I would tell them that their old one did it too. They would wonder why the other salesperson didn't tell them, and I would tell them that he didn't know. When you study your business, it will put you way ahead of your competitors.

Did you ever wonder why so many famous people seem to lead unhappy lives? Everywhere you look, magazines and books tell stories of heartbreaks of the rich and famous. They are checking into drug and alcohol rehabilitation centers, and their third or fourth or fifth marriages are breaking up. These people fulfill their dreams of being movie stars, great entertainers, and rock stars. They had the desire and determination to stick it out until they reached their dream. When they made it to the top, they were still unhappy. Their success did not give them the happiness that they thought it would. Money can't buy you happiness, but it will help with lots of things, and you have to have it. Whatever service you do, do it with passion—serve your customers and love what you do. People who have a crusade have an extra edge in life. They hang on to their dreams when the rest of us get tired and stop. They have inner strength and toughness that can't be duplicated in any other way. A dream backed up by a crusade is an almost unstoppable combination. Crusaders are always on a mission. When I got into sales, I wanted to make a difference and add value to the customer's situation. I always feel that I have the best product for their situation, and I will always show them I do. Remember that you work for them; they don't work for you. A crusade, simply put, is something that's bigger than you are. It's a cause with an impact that reaches beyond your personal wants and needs. In a dog-eat-dog business world, a lot of people think that the old moral values and principles just don't apply anymore. They think that the Christian principles taught in the Bible are stale and outdated, but crusaders stand for something. They know that how you live and how you conduct your business are more important than the bottom line. They believe that honesty and integrity are priorities, and they recognize that no cause is worth crusading for if it is not built on a basis of goodness and rightness. So anytime you are in the presence of your customer, show them a loving atmosphere. Show them why you have the best service for them, and prove it. Know what your competitors are doing, and outdo them. Turn your business into a crusade, and outlive (happy life), outwork, outlove, outstudy, and outlast your competition. You can do this, and we will do this together!

Chapter 3

Be Genuine

Be Yourself

Being a professional salesperson, it is easy to find a presentation that's already made, and that's fine. The trouble is when you sound like you are reading it right off the paper. When you are learning your presentation or any part of the sales process, it needs to sound genuine. I have also seen outstanding salespeople do really well, and I have seen other newer salespeople try to be like them. Be yourself—whatever you learn, learn to make it match your personality. To make it match, you have to practice. I like to practice in the mirror, over and over again. When you first greet a customer, it is their first impression of you, so make sure you nail it. If you sound like you know what you are talking about, you have a better chance of getting the sale. If there is something you don't know, tell them, and let them know you will find out. You see, people are looking to see if you are being real with them or not. Please don't fail the test; they might ask you something that they already know the answer to, so just tell the truth about anything they may ask.

Buying is an emotional process and often an impulse. That's why your enthusiasm is critical, from the greeting throughout your selling and closing process. You can help build their emotions even more in your presentation, but only if you know their emotional hot buttons, which you can find through rapport and an investigation process. You can keep their emotions running high if you know how to ask the right questions at the right time, how to use the positive assumptive statement about how and when they will use it, and how to talk past the sales and create mental ownership. The selling process will help you get the customer to feel comfortable working with you. To give you an example of a sales process: (1) meet and greet (2) consultation (3) your product, the demo (show time), and then the close. You will need to perfect each step. Don't cheat yourself, because this is where the money is made. Most companies have their own process, or you can create your own if they don't. Your process guides you through investigating so that you will know every hot button they have. Then the steps of selling will walk you through a great demo presentation and straight into an effective closing sequence.

Being genuine is just being yourself. Whatever you learn in the world of sales, apply it to your personality. Don't ever try to be someone else. Remember, learn from other people; don't try to be them. In sales, customers buy you—that's right, you—so be the best you can be. Genuine things are true or authentic. When you're about people, being genuine has to do with being sincere. This word has to do with things and people that are true. A genuine friend is a real friend. If something is genuine, it is real and exactly what it appears to be. Why do I spend so much time on this? That's a good question. You see, in this day and time, people are wiser. You can't fool people anymore. I never believed in telling people anything anyway; that never was in my DNA. So, as a sales professional, be real and be yourself. As you learn to master this, you will see your sales go to a level that you did not know was there. People will recommend you to their friends and family.

People will notice just by talking to you that you are the one to do business with. Sometimes people will tell me that they tried sales but were too honest. WHAT? You see, people have tied sales and lying together. WRONG! If a salesperson (if he or she is lying, he or she is not a professional) has to lie, they have not been properly trained. You do not have to lie in the world of sales—if someone tells you to do that, look for the nearest exit. I think you get the picture on being yourself and being genuine—it's very important. Work on just being aware of what you are doing and saying. Being a sales professional, you need every edge you can have, and it all comes together in the end. These methods and principles that I am talking about in this book have been tried and proven, so master them. We will talk about this more in the upcoming chapters.

I want you to take this book as a guide and a reference for when you need motivation and guidance. You see, when the world tries to lock you down as average, telling you that you only should make minimum wage and that you should be happy, I want you to know that there is a professional sales position waiting for you. When you learn the profession of selling, you can go anywhere. Selling is entrepreneurship. You can be a barber, or sell clothing, stocks, or anything, and this book will apply. You can come into the world of sales and make a good life for yourself and your family. Take a stand. If you are dissatisfied with your current circumstances, admit that no one can fix them except you. It doesn't do any good to blame the economy, your boss, your spouse, or your family. Change can only occur when you make a conscious decision to make it happen. Make a decision; make it happen!

Don't Lie

Wow, this is a good one. There's an old myth that says that you have to be a good liar to be a good professional. Now, that is a lie. In sales, training is so important, and when it comes to training, you train all the time, but you never learn it all. The salesperson that lies, never shoots straight with you. They don't last; they are here this week and somewhere else the next. They never build a solid foundation anywhere. Those are the ones you don't want to be like. You can learn some good things from them, but that selling style does not work for the long haul. Most of the general public thinks that if you are in business, you have to be a crook. This is not true, but every time you greet a customer, the customer is looking for you to tell them a lie before it's all over. Now, as a sales professional, you need to keep that in mind at all times. WHY? Because when you do everything you should do, and you do it right, you will earn that person's trust for a lifetime.

Don't ever put yourself in a position where you have to tell a lie to get out of it—I promise that the customer will be waiting to catch you. Make it a habit to do and say the right things. A lie is a false statement made with deliberate intent to deceive—an intentional untruth, a falsehood, something intended or serving to convey a false impression (lying). Stay away from that. That is a career killer. I have seen salespeople lie and think they are doing something, and they never last long. Somebody has told them that lying was part of the business—WRONG. When you are being honest with your customers, they know it and appreciate it.

When you become an entrepreneur, remember that you are competing for business, as well as to have customers tell other people to go see "Joe" because they can trust him. You need your customer talking like that about you to the public. Customers today have more choices than ever to choose from. The challenge is to persuade each customer that your service is superior to your competition. You do that by showing them the value of your service every time you come in contact with them in person or on the phone. Let them know that you have no reason to lie to them about anything. A customer expects only a few things: They want a good deal (a good deal is all in the mind); they want you to be straight with them; and they want you to appreciate their business.

Think about the service you receive from other industries. How does your opinion about the service change when you know that they are thankful to have you as a customer? The same goes for your customers. Most people don't wake up in the morning excited about coming to your place of business. So if you can put a smile on their face as they leave, even if it's just a small smile, the customer will remember the feeling for a long time. The general rule of thumb is that a customer with a bad experience will tell 12 people. If the customer had a satisfactory or mediocre experience, they will keep it to themselves. But if the customer has an unexpectedly good experience, they will typically tell two or three others. Because of today's competitive market for any type of service, being good enough is no longer good enough. Add a little gift for your customer, and make them smile. As a professional salesperson, I can say that I have had customers drive 3 hours to come do business with me. That means they drove by 100 or more dealerships to do business with me. WHY? Because I let them know up front that I will not lie to them, and that I will give the best deal and am working for them. I also tell them that I will be their car agent when it comes to their vehicle or any vehicle, and for them to call me. When you know you are doing the right thing, and you are doing the customer right, you will always feel good about what you do.

To sum it up, be truthful with your customer; don't lie to them. The reason I repeat some things is because I believe repetition and competition equal high commission. So when you hear something over and over, there is a reason. At the beginning of this book, I talked about the fundamentals. When I see an awesome football player (NFL), I wonder how many times they practiced that play before they got it right. Former NFL players will tell you that they run some plays hundreds of times. In regard to the things to do in this book, do them over and over until you win.

I Will Get Back to You

"I will get back to you" is one of the biggest lies most sales people tell every day. "I will get back to you" is one of the easiest ways to get rid of a customer. It's not about a sale; most of the time, it's a customer that had problems and needs some attention. We call them "problem customers." If you tell a customer that you will get back to them, do exactly what you say you were going to do. Sometimes they are not problem customers. Sometimes they are hard customers to sell—they ask the crazy questions, and it is months and sometimes a year or more before they are ready to make a purchase—but they will buy. I can't tell you how many times customers like this come into the business asking some of the same questions that they asked last time. The salesperson doesn't take them seriously, but six months later, you will see them at another salesperson's desk, ready to do business. You never know; the problem customer might want an upgrade soon, so don't push these customers to the side.

There will be a lots of times when you are in a hurry and will have to tell them that you will get back to them, and that's fine— just get back to them. It goes back to what we talked about in the early chapters, when you need to just be truthful to all customers. Treat people well, no matter what your business or career is; you can't do it alone. The more success you have, the more likely it is that you will have other people on your success team. How you treat those people can make the difference in whether your business takes off or falls flat. You must treat them with honesty and integrity before you can expect them to treat you in the same way. You can be great in all the areas we have talked about so far—have great desire, have a big dream, be a crusader, have a great attitude—and still fail if you don't understand human nature. But before you can develop the art of people management, you may have to make some changes in your outlook.

You must believe in the goodness of people. Before you can be successful, you must believe in the goodness of people. Unfortunately, most people don't. Most people have been so hurt and disappointed by other salespeople that they just can't believe that human beings have the potential to be good. Instead, they say that everybody's out to cheat them and take advantage of them. People are skeptical of everybody and everything. As you can see, different people look at things differently—you might think they are thinking red, but they are thinking blue. It's your responsibility to find out. It's not hard; just listen to the customer, and they will tell you everything, which is a good thing. If they believe everything you say, then why can't you do what you say? It's not hard, but we make it hard because we will say anything to a customer to get rid of them if they are not buying soon enough.

As sales professionals, our customer service should be top notch compared to your competition. When a customer has a problem, deal with it. In the long haul, you will be glad you did. They are coming to you for answers. You are the professional—show them you are. When a customer is asking you questions, they know when you are putting them off—they feel it—so don't do that. To sum this up, get back to them; it's something they need to know, and they feel that they can get the answer from you. They see you as the professional—just see yourself the same way they do. I have had this type of customer all the time. When I get back to them and let them know what they need to know, lots of times they have a family member that needs my service. You never know; a customer knows lots of prospects, and those prospects will turn into income. Just do what you say you will do; treat everyone with respect, and they will pay you. You see, everybody gets the red carpet treatment—everybody. If you do that, you don't have to worry about a thing. Remember, people want to feel special. Make them feel special, because they are special. Always put your customer first. Let them know that you appreciate them: "When I say that I will get back to you, I mean that I will get back to you, because you are very special to me and my family." If you master this, you are on your way to six figures.

Nothing to Hide

When a customer comes to your place of business, most of the time they think you are not going to be real with them. The public has put salespeople down for so long that they think it's not a reality that a salesperson wants to be truthful to them. This means that you have to show them that you can tell the truth, and that you are working for them. Once you do that, you can make something happen for them. Learn how to be compassionate for your customer. Listen to them. They will tell you what their needs are, if you just listen. Compassion is rare and only shown by a very few. We overlook the everyday kindness that we give because of our compassionate nature. We take it for granted, being kind to someone. Compassion is sympathetic pity and concern for the sufferings or misfortunes of others. Sell your service from the heart. Make your career a crusade. Treat people as you want them to treat you. No matter what your business is, you can't do it alone. The more success you have, the more likely it is that you will have other people on your success team. How you treat those people can make the difference in whether your business takes off or fails. You must treat them with honesty and integrity before you can expect them to treat you in the same way.

Listening is a great skill to learn. Most people think that to be good in sales, you need to be talking—WRONG!!! Lots of talking will turn a customer off. Don't get me wrong; there are times when you need to talk but not all the time. When it is time to talk, know what you are talking about, and make sure you are responding to the customer's needs. Listening is giving one's attention to sound or action. A way to improve your listening skills is to practice active listening. This is where you make a conscious effort to hear not only the words that another person is saying, but more importantly, the complete message being communicated. How well do you listen? If you learn to listen well, you will close more deals. The customer knows when you are not listening to them. When you listen, the customer notices it, and you look more credible to them. When you earn their trust, they will be ready to do business with you, and only you. Always be an open book to your customers about the products. Let them know that you have nothing to hide. If you learn to do these things, you will put sales professional's careers on another level. You see, when you are training yourself, your competition is sleeping. Always work on your selling skills.

When you are a true professional, the customer knows it, and that is what they want to see. Trust is a firm belief in the reliability, truth, ability, or strength of someone. The idea that a business needs to treat its customers well, and really understand their likes, dislikes, and habits, is so obvious that it seems hardly worth stating. But oddly enough, many people in business fail in this area. *"There is only one boss—the customer—and he can fire everybody in the company, from the chairman on down, simply by spending his money somewhere else."* – Sam Walton Fundamentally, you are in business to utilize the assets that you have, to generate a positive return on your hard work (the work you put in training). Your return will be a higher income. To accomplish this, you will sell a product or service to your customers, and hopefully earn a profit on each transaction. It's really that simple. So why do many professionals take their customers for granted? To know what it's like to be buying a product from you or your company, you have to put yourself in the shoes of the customer. Sadly, few professionals really get the concept.

To sum it up, just do right by your customer. Let them know that you are on their side and that you work for them. When you listen to a customer, find out their needs, and then show them why your product or service will fit their needs perfectly. When you do it the right way, you will have a customer for life!

Respect Your Customer

Respect is another small word with a big meaning. When you are in the business world, you will find out that people easily get angry about anything. During a transaction, you need to ask if everything is going okay so far. That way, you will know that things are going fine, and it will make them feel respected as well.

Respect, esteem, admire, think highly of, have a high opinion of, hold in high regard, and make your customer comfortable. I have seen sales professionals be disrespectful to customers, where they did not know that the customer's feelings were hurt. If you pay attention to them, you will be fine. I remember a time when a salesperson sold a car to a young college professor. The professor was so excited about the purchase. He had to come back for floor mats. On the day he came back for the mats, his salesperson was very busy as he was a great salesperson. The professor waited a little too long for someone to get him the mats. The salesperson checked on him but did not give him full attention. Well, when the professor got the survey in the mail (the survey is where the customer gets to grade the salesperson and the company), he gave them a low grade. With some companies, if your survey score falls below company average, you lose bonus money. I know that will get your attention. It doesn't have to come to that; just take care of your customer. Now, some customers can be a little overbearing, but don't let that bother you—just remember to close the deal and earn the business. Anytime that you are in the middle of a business transaction, be aware of the customer's state of mind. Being aware will allow you to navigate through the transaction and stay in control of the situation. Just stay on track, and always try to think what the customer is thinking. This can be hard sometimes, but if you practice customer service skills, and learn to listen, it will become a little easier for you. Being a sales professional, in any industry, you want that customer for life. You have to love what you do, and this will put you in the 6-figure income bracket. Learn what you love doing, treat people right, and the universe will take care of the rest (I know, some of you didn't get that).

I have seen salespeople who have bad attitudes—they don't last long. Attitudes just bleed right out into your personality. If you don't like dealing with people, sales is not for you, but you can change.

Respecting your customer is about giving your all while they are with you. That's not hard to do, and they will reward you well. I remember a salesperson that was on the same sales team with me, about 10 years ago, and he had a short temper. He came in on his day off; he needed a sale. The customer showed up 3 hours late. Not only was he late, he showed up with an unrealistic proposal. The salesperson lost it. He said, "I come in on my day off, you show up 3 hours late, and you bring me this?" Wow...he went off. This will happen sometimes, but you have to keep your cool and be respectful. I have had that happen to me. Let me tell you what I did. First, I asked the customer where they got those numbers. I wanted to play it down a little. I let him know that I would be back. I didn't want to embarrass him. Sometimes a family member might be with them, and they don't want to look bad in front of them. When I came back, I gave them my numbers and let them know that their numbers were very unreasonable. At that point, that is all you can do, and 8 out of 10 times, they will go with your proposal. You can't get angry—you will want to, but you need to work for the sale. To sum it up, treat everybody the way you want to be treated. If someone's mother comes to your business, treat them like they are your mother. The same goes with a brother, sister, and so on—don't look down on customers. Show them the utmost respect—RESPECT, RESPECT, RESPECT, RESPECT, RESPECT, RESPECT, RESPECT!!!!!!!!!!! Please, it is that important.

Be an Agent

This is something I came up with. There are all kinds of insurance agents, real estate agents, and so on. One thing I like to do, with whatever I am doing, is to be an agent of that thing. When I sold t-shirts, I would tell people to let me be their t-shirt agent. Anything that had to do with t-shirts—any t-shirt needs—I was their man. People would laugh when I said that, but they remembered me when it came to t-shirts. In business, whenever your product comes up in a conversation, you want your name to be synonymous with your product. When I worked as an insurance agent, I learned the true meaning of being an agent. When it comes to insurance, they depend on you for everything. If something happens, and they don't know what is covered, you need to know. When you tell them that everything is covered, the relief that comes over their face is priceless, and they will love you for life. So, whatever business you do, be the agent. I would tell them that when it comes to insurance, "Don't worry, just call me." It takes all the pressure off them, and they love that. If you do all the right things, they will put all their trust in you. They will send you business for life. People just want a good product and to be treated right. Whatever product I am selling, just call me; I will take care of the rest. After you sell your product, your customer goes home, and you want them to feel like they got the best product, the best deal, and the best agent—I have no worries. As an agent, you have to pride yourself on taking care of your customers. I love taking care of my customers and knowing my product.

I had been in the automotive industry for 17 years. I would say to someone that I wanted to be their car agent, and yes, they would laugh, but guess what? I became their car agent. I knew a family out of Florida, and you could tell that they came from the educational field (mother and father). They had two daughters that graduated from FAMU, but their job offers were in Macon, Georgia. They came to my place of business and told me the situation. I said, "Okay, sir, let me tell you what I do. If you do business with me, and your daughters have any problems, all they need to do is call me. When you are home from Florida, you don't have to worry; I will take care of them. So, sir, on your way back home tonight, just know that with your two vehicle purchases, you also get an agent. If you or they have any problems, just call." He said, "Man, I have been to three places, and I didn't feel good about any of them. Let's look at some vehicles and get this done."

People want to know whether you will be there after the sale. He got both vehicles from me that day, and we stayed in touch. Sell your product, and make friends. The old saying is true: *People don't care how much you know until they know how much you care.* Be genuine, be real with people, and learn how to help. I have seen salespeople just go right at the sales and turn the customer off. Listen to your customer. I knew by listening to the father from Florida that his daughters were his heart. I knew that he would die for them; so I also knew that my presentation needed to be about his girls in Macon, and about him in Florida. When a customer comes to your business, they will tell you what they want, but you need the skill of listening.

I hope you get the concept of being an agent. It's about taking all of the pressure off of the customer and putting it on yourself. For example, they say that they want your best price: "Okay, that's fine; I will get that for you." You want to let them know that you are not the one that is going to make this hard for them. You have to learn the non-confrontational sales process. Let them know that the only thing they have to do is call you—you are their agent.

Chapter 4

Develop a Plan

An Appropriate and Clear Plan

Anytime you design a plan, you want it to be clear and attainable. You might say that you want to make a six-figure salary this year. Six-figure what? You would say it like this: I will make a six-figure income this year. You can see the difference: I used *will* and *income*. When you speak into your life, the universe (God) wants you to speak clear and direct. The next thing is to plan how you get to the six figures. I will talk about that in the next chapter, about finding a road map. Develop an action plan composed of action steps that address all proposed changes. Additionally, the action plan should include information and ideas you have already gathered while brainstorming about your objectives and strategies. Developing an action plan can help change-makers turn their vision into a reality, and to increase efficiency and accountability within a home and an organization.

An action plan describes the way you or your organization will meet its objectives through detailed action steps that describe how and when those steps will be taken. In some ways, an action plan is a heroic act—it's you turning your dreams into reality. An action plan is a way to make sure that you or your organization's vision is made clear and concrete. It describes the way you or your group will use its strategies to meet its objectives. An action plan consists of a number of action steps or changes to be brought to you or your organization. An action plan must be complete, clear, and current.

Complete: Does it list all of the action steps or changes to get you or your group to your objectives?

Clear: Is it apparent who will do what and by when?

Current: Does the action plan reflect the current work? Does it anticipate newly emerging opportunities and barriers?

I don't want you to get too deep in an action plan, but you will need a very good one. I have seen some sales professionals take all day on a plan. You don't want the plan to work you; you want to work the plan.

Here is a good reason why you should develop a plan. There is an old saying: People don't plan to fail; instead, they fail to plan. Because you certainly don't want to fail, it makes sense to take all of the steps necessary to ensure success, including an action plan. An action plan shows you or your organization that you are dedicated to getting things done. A plan will help you to not overlook any of the details. A plan will help you to understand what is and what isn't possible for you or your organization to do. Remember though, an action plan is always a work in progress. You must make changes as current situations change—maybe once a month. Review your completed action plan carefully to check for completeness. Make sure that each proposed change will help accomplish your or your organization's mission. Follow through; one of the challenging parts is to finish and stay on track. Take your plan and run with it! Remember the 80/20 rule: Successful efforts are 80% follow-through on planned actions, and 20% planning for success. Keep track so that you can measure your success. Work on it, and you will see that it will be one of your road maps to being successful.

Navigate Your Way to Success in Sales

Back in the old days, when I was a child, my parents would use road maps and go anywhere in the country, and you can still get road maps in most places if you want them. Now we have something called *navigation*. You put an address in, and it will take you there–WOW! This is the way your plan should be. In the early part of this book, I talked about lots of do's and don'ts. I talked about treating your customers like they should be treated—more on the customer service side of professional selling—which is very important. As I get to the middle and the last part of the book, I will talk about you getting yourself ready. We will talk about some ideas and strategies.

When you find your spot (your industry), and you start in your profession, or maybe you are already in it, you will have to learn how to navigate your side of the business to be successful. When your personal life is not in line, you have to leave it outside in an imaginary trash can. When it's game time, get focused, and stay that way until that day is over. Don't bring any negativity to your spot. Let me tell you what I mean about your spot. Your spot is where you will be doing your business from. It could be an insurance company, real estate, automotive, clothing—whatever you do or decide to do. I will talk about finding your spot, later in the book.

When you are naturally a glass-half-empty kind of person, thinking positively can make you feel a little different, but if you are a glass-half-full kind of person, you understand how to think positive. Lots of people who see the negative side of things also tend to put themselves down, because they set huge, intimidating goals that are difficult to attain. Set attainable goals, and start small; the satisfaction from reaching those smaller goals will motivate you to reach the next one. Turn problems into challenges. Words are very powerful. Try creating a list of negative words and phrases that you use often, and replace them with ones that are a bit more positive. If you regularly complain of problems, for example, start referring to them as challenges instead.

Adopt a positive mindset. People who are naturally negative tend to use "no" as their first response to new ideas and experiences. In part, they do this to buy time while actually making a decision, but then they end up defending the "no" choice and sticking to it, even at times when they might not have. You can see how that works, and you can have those negative habits also. As a professional salesperson, you will have to deal with this and handle your own negative habits and emotions. As a salesperson, your state of mind needs to be on point at all times. This is what I mean when I talk about your road map and navigating. Every time a customer sits in front of you, it's game time; listen, and they will tell you just how to sell them. Overcome the objections with soft objections at first. As you get into the closing process, you can go with some hard closes. Be careful with the hard closes; learn to make them sound soft. I will talk about hard and soft closes, later in the book.

To become successful in professional sales, you have to learn to control the whole sales process. You have to do this without the customer knowing it. Most customers want you to take control. I talked about trust earlier; when you get the trust, you get control. At that time, you know that the customer wants you to navigate your way through the bull, and let them know what you can do for them, as well as let them know that it's the best deal. Each customer has different objections to overcome. Listen to every customer, and put your game plan together as you listen and get the sale.

Attainable Plans

We will be talking a lot about planning and setting goals. When putting your plan together, make sure that it is reachable. Set it high but reachable. Where will you be in the next ten years? Where will you be in the next two or five years? Well, you can have a two-year plan and a five-year plan. What about a daily plan? I have seen people really complicate this process. Just keep it simple.

The first and most important step to take toward working more efficiently is to have a daily plan in place. Having a written plan is a must to keep nagging thoughts out of the back of your head, and to help prevent disasters because you forgot about something important. If you arrive at work each day and are immediately overwhelmed with your to-do list (you must have a to-do list), and your desk is cluttered, at best, you will bolt into your day like a racehorse (and quickly burn out after a sprint, just like a racehorse), focusing on whatever seems most pressing at any given time. The worst case is that you will sit in a funk, not knowing where to start—either way, simply putting out fires.

Without a plan, the day's distractions will quickly take over: the phone rings, you start to answer emails, co-workers start to chit-chat, and before you know it, lunchtime has arrived and you have little accomplished. Your daily plan might include an hour each morning to get settled by returning calls and checking emails, before you get started on other tasks. If you purposely set aside an hour to do something, and you go over that time limit, you will know that you need to adjust your plan for the next day.

I like to attack my day. Before you head off to work, decide ahead of time what you will focus on when you get there. Plan your day the night before, and prepare your desk for the task you want to accomplish in the morning. For example, get files or reading material organized for the morning so that you can jump right in, or put items you need to type, or phone calls you need to return, in the order in which you need to get them done. Having a plan can help you create predictable routines, which will in turn keep you better prepared to face chaotic days, when your boss or a high maintenance client demands more of your time. I will say it again: Keep it simple. Tailor your plan to match you and your profession. Keep a to-do list, and plan your day.

If you work your daily plan, which is the foundation of the long-term plan, you will see how well and how fast things come together. When you are putting together a long-term plan, you need to consider where you want to be financially. Know yourself; keep data on yourself. I have files right now where I can tell you who I sold to in May 2010. I can tell you what month of the year is traditionally my best month. I know how many applications it takes for me to get to the sale. If I want to be at a certain level financially, I know what I need to do. Learn this about yourself and your profession. A good fisherman can tell what month the fish are biting, what kind of fish are biting, and what bait to use. What kind of fisherman are you? Do you know what it takes for you to get the sale? I can't tell you how important these things are. They're like nuggets of gold to your professional career, and you will find out that this is a successful road map to a great financial career. If you want to make a six-figure income, find out what it will take for you. Just start keeping data on yourself, and watch the magic begin to happen. We will be talking about goals in the upcoming chapters. Goals and plans are similar, but goals are something you are passionate about, and something you genuinely want to achieve in your life or business. You don't just expect things to happen—make things happen. The plan is put in place to reach that goal step by step. GET YOUR PLAN IN PLACE, AND WIN BIG!!!!!!

Time to Work on Your Plan

This can be tricky. I have seen people work on their plan so hard and for so long, they spend more and more time working on the plan than acting on the plan. The financial section of your business plan determines whether or not your business idea is viable, and will be the focus of any investors who may be attracted to your business ideas. You don't have to have investors, but if someone is interested, it is worth taking a look at it. The financial section is composed of three financial statements: the income statement, the cash flow projection, and the balance sheet, and the brief analysis of these three statements. You don't have to complicate these statements; make them as simple as you can. Whatever way works for you, that is what you stay with. Before you begin, however, you must gather the financial data that you will need, including all of your expenses.

A good business plan can help you get your thoughts organized. It can provide a guideline so that you are not stuck looking at a blank page and trying to figure out where to start; plus it shows you the general layout of a standard business plan so that you know what goes where, and that you are not leaving out anything. When you are serious about your business, even if you don't have anything down in writing, you have already started to plan. So how do you find time to write a business plan? You don't. You are always planning. Your plan is never done, but your planning process is the key to good management. Your plan is for you first. Don't make it for anyone else. Do it because it helps you divide and manage big goals into practical steps. Instead of looking at it as a document, think of your business plans as a place on your computer where you collect ideas, useful stories, lists, and numbers. It's a place where you keep track of the market, your milestones, goals, and projections. Planning is a process that includes review and revision. There is always the latest version, and it lasts just a few months.

Things to consider as milestones: what's supposed to happen, when, and who is responsible. Basic numbers: simple spreadsheet projections for sales, cost, and expenses.

Strategy: deciding how to focus a business offering on key target market. It can start with just bullet points. I have seen it done well with pictures. It is mostly a reminder for you and your team.

Cash flow: Because profits don't guarantee enough cash to pay bills, you need to manage cash from the beginning. Month by month, account for what you spend and what you deposit—not profit as it appears on the books, but money as it shows in the bank.

Review schedule: Set aside time for a plan versus actual review, once a month, to compare what you planned would happen. Be brief and practical.

Keep track of these main elements, and grow your plan organically as your business grows. By recording what is supposed to happen, you will be able to better manage why, when, and how things go wrong. You will be able to set performance metrics and develop accountability for different tasks and milestones. Again, don't complicate this; keep it simple. Remember, it is for you—tailor-made for you—it is to fit you only.

The best time of the day for you to concentrate on your plan is early in the morning or late at night. I prefer the morning, while the mind is fresh and there are no disturbances—get this done, and watch how fast your business grows!

Write It Down (the Plan)

Just write it down. This title refers to two things: the extra task you are using to procrastinate, and the words that are in your mind that need to be etched somewhere physical. That piece of writing that you have sitting in that notebook or document is not going to write itself.

It's time to do some prioritizing. Do you really need to get those goals done, or are you just actively procrastinating? This is not to make you feel guilty but to just make you productive. I am the first to admit that I do this. We all do this.

Finishing something feels good, and it motivates you to continue. If you are stalled right now, then this is a way to give yourself some momentum. Stop trying to edit while you write. This is not school. No one is going to stamp your plan with a giant red "F." And if they do, then you can always improve it. Writing is not dead once it reaches the paper; it can change. Stop trying to find that perfect word. Leave that for later, when you go back to edit your plan. This does not have to be the single greatest work you have produced. It's probably not going to be, but that doesn't mean that you do not have an obligation to write it down anyway.

Just write down as much as you can remember; the plan is for you. A published book gets revised many times. You can always go back and make changes. Even in Habakkuk 2:2, it says, "Then the Lord replied, 'Write my answer plainly on tablets, so that a runner can carry the correct message to others.'" As you can see, writing things down is an old and effective method that works.

Most people drive through life without bothering to write down their plans. Very few people have specific and measurable goals, and even fewer have written these goals down. Does writing down your goals really help, or is it just a myth? If it really helps, what's the best goal/plan setting strategy? Forbes reports a remarkable study about goals/plans setting, carried out in the Harvard MBA program. Harvard graduate students were asked if they had set clear and written goals for their future, as if they had made specific plans to transform their fantasies into realities. The result of the study was that only 3% of the students had written goals and plans to accomplish them; 13% had goals/plans in their minds but had not written them anywhere; and 84% had no goals/plans at all. What group would you belong to? After 10 years, the same group of students were interviewed again, and the conclusion of the study was totally astonishing. The 13% of the class, who had goals but did not write them down, earned twice the amount of the 84% who had no goals/plans. The 3% who had written goals/plans were earning, on an average, 10 times as much as the other 97% of the class combined. People who do not write down goals tend to fail easier than the ones who have plans. When you do not have a plan, you do not know how you will reach your destination.

All winners get up early every day. All winners have a routine. Let's look at the word, *routine*: a sequence of actions regularly followed; a fixed program. In your early morning routine, make sure you read your plan. You may have a long written plan, but you can condense your plan for the morning routine and always keep it in mind. Doing this will keep you on track and motivated.

We all know the importance of starting our day by eating a healthy breakfast. A proper breakfast provides your body with the fuel it needs to function well into the night. It's just as important to start your business day right by starting with your daily planning session. It will provide you with the fuel you need to make the most out of your business day.

A daily planning session of just 20–30 minutes will let you focus on your business plan, and energize yourself for the day ahead. Spending this time organizing yourself at the start of the day will save you time during the day. Your daily planning session is your chance to review your progress on the specific business plans/goals you have set. Set your daily agenda, and prioritize your tasks for the day. Getting your day organized, and knowing that you are focused on achieving the business plan/goals you have set for yourself, will give you an edge on the competitor. To pack even more of a punch to your daily planning session, include an inspirational moment in each session. I like to read and reflect on an inspirational quote from a successful person, or a quote from the Bible, each day. It gives me positive motivation for my day ahead.

Your daily planning session needs to be uninterrupted. Do not take phone calls during this time. When you are setting your daily agenda, put your most demanding task into your most productive working times. For example, if you are a morning person, schedule whatever creative tasks you need to accomplish, in the morning rather than into the late afternoon, when your mental energy is low.

A quick way to prioritize is to highlight the 3 or 4 most important tasks of the day. It's not necessary to obsessively order tasks to get a sense of what's most important that day. Resist the temptation to grade yourself on your performance of your daily agenda. If you don't accomplish all the tasks you have listed for that day, it does not mean you have failed; it just means you did not accomplish everything on your list.

As you take on your day, just keep in mind what your plan is for that day. Learn to stay on task. I have a trigger point. When I find myself getting off task, my trigger point is to talk to myself. I tell myself to get on task and to stay on task. I say it over and over until I get focused again. I know that sounds a little weird, but it works.

Chapter 5

Set Goals

By now, you can see that goals and planning are very important. Chapters 4 and 5 are all about setting goals and planning. Many people feel as if they are adrift in the world. They work hard, but they don't seem to get anywhere worthwhile. First consider what you want to achieve, and then commit to it. Set smart, specifically measurable, attainable, relevant, and time-bound goals that motivate you, and write them down to make them feel tangible. Then plan the steps you must take to realize your goals, and cross off each one as you work through them.

Goal setting is a powerful process for thinking about your ideal future, and for motivating yourself to turn your vision of this future into reality. The process of setting goals helps you choose where you want to go in life. By knowing precisely what you want to achieve, you know where you have to concentrate your efforts. You will also quickly spot the distractions that can so easily lead you astray.

Why set goals? Top level athletes, successful business people, and achievers in all fields, all set goals. Setting goals gives you long-term vision and short-term motivation. It focuses your acquisition of knowledge, and helps you to organize your time and your resources so that you can make the most of your life. By setting sharp, clearly defined goals, you can measure and take pride in the achievement of those goals, and you will see forward progress in what might previously have seemed a long pointless grind. You will also raise your self-confidence as you recognize your own ability and competence in achieving the goals that you have set. Start setting personal goals. You set goals on a number of levels. First, you create your big picture of what you want to do with your life (say for the next 10 years), and identify the large-scale goals that you want to achieve. Then you break these down into smaller and smaller targets that you must hit to reach your lifetime goals. Finally, once you have your plan, you start working on it to achieve those goals. This is why we start the process of setting goals by looking at your lifetime goals. Then we work down to the things that you can do in the next five years, for example, and then next year, next month, next week, and today, to start moving toward them.

Setting personal goals is to consider what you want to achieve in your lifetime. Setting lifetime goals gives you the overall perspective that shapes all other aspects of your decision-making. To give broad balanced coverage of all important areas in your life, try to set goals in some of the following categories, or in other categories of your own, where these are important to you.

Career: What level do you want to reach in your career, or what do you want to achieve? Financial: How much do you want to earn, and by what stage? How is this related to your career goals?

Education: Is there any knowledge you want to acquire in particular? What information and skills will you need to have in order to achieve educational goals?

Family: Do you want to be a parent? Some of us are already parents. If so, how are you going to be a good parent? How do you want to be seen by members of your extended family?

Attitude: Is any part of your mindset holding you back? Is there any part of the way that you behave that upsets you? If so, set a goal to improve your behavior, or find a solution to the problem.

Physical: Are there any athletic goals that you want to achieve? Do you want good health deep into old age?

We can go on, but I think you get the picture. Remember, this is for and by you, so put it together the way you want.

Attainable Goals

Setting goals is very important to being successful in the profession of sales, but you want to set attainable goals. First, consider what you want to achieve, and then commit to it. Set smart (specific, measurable, attainable, relevant, and time bound) goals that motivate you, and write them down to make them feel tangible. Then plan the steps you must take to realize your goal, and cross off each one as you work through them. Many people feel as if they are adrift in the world. They work hard, but they don't seem to get anywhere worthwhile. A key reason why they feel this way is that they have not spent enough time thinking about what they want from life, and have not set themselves formal goals. After all, would you set out on a major journey with no real idea of your destination? Probably not! Top-level athletes, successful business people, and achievers in all fields, all set goals. Setting goals gives you long-term vision and short-term motivation. It focuses your acquisition knowledge, and helps you to organize your time and your resources so that you can make the most of your life.

By setting sharp, clearly defined goals, you can measure and take pride in the achievements of those goals, and you will see forward progress in what might previously have seemed a long pointless grind. You will also raise your self-confidence as you recognize your own ability and competence in achieving the goals that you have set. You create big pictures of what you want to do with your life (say for the next 10 years), and identify the large-scale goals that you want to achieve. Then you break these down into the smaller and smaller targets that you must hit to reach your life time goals. Finally, once you have your plan, you start working on it to achieve these goals. This is why we start the process of setting goals by looking at our lifetime goals. Then we work down to the things that you can do in the next five years, then the next year, next month, next week, and day, to start moving toward them. You see, we want to keep it simple, step by step.

You need to know what you want and need to do for your family. What level do you want to reach in your career, or what do you want to achieve? How much do you want to earn? How is this related to your career goals? Is there any knowledge you want to acquire in particular? What information and skills will you need to have in order to achieve other goals? Is any part of your mindset holding you back? Spend some time brainstorming these things, and then select one or more goals in each category that best reflects what you do. Then consider trimming again so that you have a small number of really significant goals that you can focus on. As you do this, make sure that the goals that you have set are ones that you genuinely want to achieve, not ones that your parents, family, or employers might want. Create a one-year plan, a six-month plan, and a one-month plan of progressively smaller goals that you should reach to achieve your lifetime goals. Each of these should be based on the previous plan. Create a daily to-do list of things that you should do today to work toward your lifetime goals. At an early stage, your smaller goals might be to read and gather information on the achievement of your higher-level goals. This will help you to improve the quality and realism of your goal setting.

Finally, review your plans, and make sure that they fit the way that you want to live your life. So you see, it's all about planning. Put together a plan, work the plan, and be successful in anything you do!!!

Write Them Down

In the earlier chapters, I talked about writing the plan down. Now we are talking about writing the goals down. When you write down your ideas, you automatically focus your full attention on them. Only a few, if any of us, can write one thought and think another at the same time. This is when pencil and paper make excellent concentration tools. Have you ever heard the saying that a dull pencil is better than a sharp mind? Write down a thought at the moment. Those that come unsought are commonly the most valuable. One of the simplest but most powerful habits I have established in my life in the past few years is to write things down more often. I have also noticed, when reviewing old notes, how much my memory can leak. The memory is not very reliable. Sometimes we recreate what happened rather than just replay a film from our mental archives. The recreation is directed by a number of things, such as our belief and our emotional state at the time. What you remember about an event may differ quite a bit from what someone else remembers. There is a wide variety of interpretations of reality, and then when you try to remember that interpretation of an event later on, it can change even more. So, we need some kind of system, outside of ourselves.

Ideas don't stay for long. Awesome ideas can pop up at the strangest times, but they tend to not stay for long in your head. So you need to capture them fast, or they are gone in the wind. Written goals are very important. A lot of very successful improvement writers, like Anthony Robbins, Brian Tracy, Zig Ziglar, and so on, teach this in all of their workshops. I could go on and on about the importance of having written goals, only to reaffirm what your goals are. You may also find insights that bring more clarity and focus to your goals and your life.

A written goal is also a powerful reminder that you can use to keep yourself on the right track, when you feel stressed and might consider making a hasty decision. Remind yourself of what to focus on. Often, we get caught up in our everyday business, and we lose track of what is most important. To keep yourself on track, instead of just keeping yourself busy with low-priority tasks, simply write down a reminder that can stop your thoughts when you see it, and guide you back on track again. I also like reminders such as, "Is this useful," and "what is the most important thing I can do right now?" Write down your reminders, and put that reminder where you can't avoid seeing it throughout your day. You cannot hold that many thoughts in your head at once. If you want to solve a problem, it can be helpful to write down your thoughts, facts, and feelings about it. Then you don't have to use your mind for remembering; you can instead use it (the mind) to think more clearly. Having it all written down gives you an overview and makes it easier to find new connections that can help you solve the problem.

Writing things down enables a higher level of thinking and, therefore, more focused action. When your brain is not busy remembering everything, your brain can process anything. For this reason, writing things down can help our brains prioritize what we should focus on and act on at any given moment. Write your goals down, and watch the magic it creates for your business!!!

Keep Them on You

We all know how powerful it is to write your goals down. It is a good idea to keep them on you at all times, in some type of condensed form. I condensed my goals on an index card so that I could look at it from time to time during the day. Some people think that you should keep your goals to yourself. That is simply up to you and how you want to handle that. Some people love to tell people about their goals—again, that is up to you.

Keeping your goals in front of you is very important. Some very successful people advocate writing and rewriting your goals every day. Others say that it's good enough to just read them each day. The basic idea is to keep refreshing your goals in your mind so that you think about them often. If you don't employ such a practice, it's easier to lose sight of your goals. You get caught up in day-to-day activities, and the most important long-term goals fall by the wayside. Instead of leading your life, you merely react to whatever comes up. When this happens to me, I start getting an empty, sinking feeling. A week goes by, and I feel like I did not really get much done, even though I may have been very busy. Unimportant tasks consume my time, and my goals don't seem to be getting any closer. Have you ever felt that way?

On the other hand, when I am very focused on my goals and am working on them actively, I feel great. I have more energy and motivation, and I end my week with a major sense of accomplishment. Some people think that motivation spawns action, but action also spawns motivation. Motivation is the feeling that comes from building and maintaining momentum. When you can see your goals getting closer from day to day, it's very energizing. There are lots of ways to keep your goals in front of you. You can create a belief board in your office or work station. Here are some other ideas to consider. Use a digital photo frame to display photos of your goals. For example, if you want to go on a vacation, put up photos of the places you want to visit. You can also create your own image affirmations (with or without background pictures), and add those to choose an inspiring desktop background. You can add a list of your top goals to your desktop background image so that they are always visible on the screen. Just load up the pictures in an image editor, add some text to it, and re-save it.

Print your goals in a large font, and post them around your home and workplace so that you can see them often. If this sort of thing would embarrass you, and if someone came in to visit and saw your goals posted everywhere, then you really need to get over yourself. Plus, you need better friends who will respect people with goals. If anything, you will be doing your visitors a big favor by reminding them to think about their goals more often too. If you can't even summon the courage to do this, then what chance do you have of achieving your goals? Tell people about your goals. Remember how I said earlier that it's your choice to tell or not. I think it's okay to share your goals with people openly. Now, when you do that, some people will support you, some will not seem to care, and other people will criticize you.

Talking about your goals is a great way to filter your friends and family, because it immediately shows you who is on your side and who is only going to hold you back. That's good information to have. It gives you advanced warning about people who are likely to go kittywampus as you get closer to your goals. For example, if you tell people that your current financial goal is to earn $10,000 per month, even though you are only making $3,000 a month right now, some people might get hypercritical just because you set that goal. They see you as a threat to their complacency and laziness, so they will poke fun at you, attack you, etc. If you start working on your goals and have a setback, they will be the first people to jump on you and call you a failure.

You need to cut those people out eventually, and the sooner the better. If they can't handle your ambitions now, imagine what it will be like when you actually hit the $10,000 a month. They want to be able to deal with it. They are just going to get worse along the way, and create a psychological drag on you that may very well make you fail. I know that I went a little long with this, but this is very important. Get them out of your life, and stick to your goals!!!

Read Them Every Day

Some of this may sound repetitive. Repetition is the road map to greatness. Have you seen a professional ball player make an awesome play? When you talk to professional athletes, they will tell you how many times the team practices a single play. The same goes for your professional business career. So, repetition is good.

Make it a habit to read your goals every day. Reading them on a daily basis is about a habit that will focus your energy and set you on a path to get what you really want out of life. It all starts as an idea that you repeat in your head, scribble on a loose piece of paper, or thoughtfully draft on a digital document. The second creation (the part we get to see) is how you bring that idea into the physical world. The stronger you make your idea, the easier it will be to bring it into reality. Those ideas turn into goals.

When you write and review your goals regularly, you will be able to live a more fulfilling and intentional life by keeping track of what you want. A quick way to prioritize is to highlight the 3 or 4 most important tasks of the day. It's not necessary to obsessively order tasks to get a sense of what's most important that day. Resist the temptation to grade yourself on your performance of your daily agenda. If you don't accomplish all the tasks you have listed for that day, it does not mean you have failed. It just means you did not accomplish everything on your list.

As you take on your day, just keep in mind what your plan is for that day. Learn to stay on task. I have a trigger point when I find myself getting off task. My trigger point is to talk to myself. I tell myself to get on task and to stay on task. I say it over and over until I get my focus back. I know that sounds a little weird, but it works.

Define and refine what you really want and need. Your goals will act as a sign post that you can reference when you are unsure of what actions you should take. A written document states your intentions in black and white, and when reviewing those intentions, it becomes obvious when you are not performing the action necessary to reach your goals, allowing you to be a better long-term decision maker. Referencing written goals allows you to think more clearly about what you want. The clear thinking will lead to better decisions. Day by day, you will be better able to consider not only the short-term benefits of your choices but also the long-term paths you would like your life to follow.

You become what you think about most of the time, and the most important part of each day is what you think about at the beginning of the day. Start your day right. I like to take 30 minutes each morning to sit and to reflect on my goals. You will find that when you read the biographies and autobiographies of successful men and women, almost every one of them began their upward trajectory to success when they began getting up early in the morning and spending time with themselves.

Goals are an important part of life. We all have them—from our finances to our careers, to our health and our relationships. Goals can run the gamut in our lives. Daily goal setting is an integral part of any successful routine because it allows us to weigh and analyze just where we start on a day-to-day basis.

The first step in setting daily goals is to know your long-term target. You can't have daily goals until you know what you are aiming for. Knowing the destination you are traveling to is much more important than knowing the direction or route to your destination. The direction and route can change or be discovered along the way, but the destination must be known. As you have seen, long-term goals are a prerequisite to short-term goals and milestones. If we don't know where we are headed, how are we supposed to make a plan to get there?

Plans and Goals Go Hand in Hand

I will be talking to you in the later chapters about the golden hour. It's the time of day when you go over your plans and goals. I know you have heard the old saying, "Keep it simple." The key is to keep it simple. Some people decide to create elaborate vision binders and what-nots, but it takes too much time and effort, so they don't maintain the habit. It's better to take 2 minutes to print and post a plan, and have it right in front of you. You can always fancy it up later if you have time.

A simple practice done regularly is superior to a complex practice done irregularly or not at all. If you can't get something in front of you in less than 5 minutes, you are overcomplicating the process. It's really not that difficult. The benefit of reading and keeping your goals in front of you every day is that you are constantly refreshing your goal-oriented mindset. You make it hard to forget about them. You may still go dark from time to time, but your reminders will create that positive pressure that says, "I'm still here, and I'm not letting you off the hook that easily." You need to make some changes and get back on track with so many things in the world. There are so many distractions these days, especially online, so this is an important practice to adopt.

One of the biggest things I see people struggling with on a day-to-day basis is keeping motivated to keep pushing forward on their goals. Is this you? Are you that person that starts really strong but then loses interest or gets distracted by other things? Or do you just need a little push to keep your major goals on the top of your mind? First, I want to congratulate you if you recognize that you need some assistance in this area. It's always about having a great mindset first, right? But then the next important thing is taking action, finding that way to shift and propel yourself into action.

As you know, planning and goal setting go hand in hand. In business, strategy and growth go hand in hand. You can create a game plan to achieve your goals, which includes a mission statement, a step-by-step strategy, and a timeline. You hold meetings, make calls, and invest. All of this planning comes together to make your goals attainable, but when you think about your personal goals, I am sure the path to achieving them looks a lot messier. It's enticing to just go with the flow rather than strategically approaching plans, especially when emotions run higher; but devising a personal growth plan can be just as valuable as creating a business plan if you truly want to reach your desired goals.

Set goals, make plans, get to work on them, stick to it, and reach your goals. The number one reason that people don't accomplish their goals is lack of genuine connection and commitment to them, but once you have figured out what you really want to do, you still need a strategy for accomplishing it. Your goals are not going to get you anywhere if you don't actually do something about them, and not just anything but the right thing. So here is a very straight forward way to get this done. Once you have done your weekly planning, you need to set aside time to plan every single day for the upcoming week. I have soaked up a ton of productive advice over the last several years, and this is something I hear from pretty much every productivity guru and successful person out there.

You have to plan on your own success. If you don't break it down to what you will do every day, then there is no way that you will accomplish your weekly, monthly, or annual goals. Basically, if you don't plan daily, you are screwed. Either you are going to own your day, or your day is going to own you!

Chapter 6

Find Your Spot

Study and Research

When finding your spot, make sure that when you get to your location, you do your research on the company, or if you are starting your own business, do your research on the business of your interest. When it was time for me to make a change from the insurance industry to the automotive industry, I did my research—lots of it. When you are looking for your spot (it's location, but I love the word spot), whatever field it may be, you want to look for a good location, with good traffic, and to study the organization from top to bottom. You want to know what kind of people you will be dealing with, and see what kind of manager is there. Have you ever heard the old saying, "Be a student of the game; be a student of your industry?"

I remember the first part of my automotive journey (the first 11 years); it had been time for a change. At that time, I was willing to travel 100 miles. I had to make up my mind: Did I want to go back to the insurance industry, or stay in the automotive industry or retail clothing (t-shirts) industry. At this time, I wanted to make sure I landed in the right place.

The reason you want to do good research is because this is where you want to be for a long time. We have to learn how to play the long game. I talked about goals and plans, and they are very important. Let me share a mistake I made by not knowing how to play the long game.

I was with a multi-level marketing company called P.F.S. I did well; some might say very well. I left the company after 10 years. That was one of the biggest mistakes I made. Why do I say that? Well, for one thing, it gave me the opportunity to make some money part time in order to build—meaning that I could build a company (my company) while I was still at my job. You build it to a producing company, leave your job, and take your company to another level. That is what this company had to offer, not knowing the long game. And what I want you to learn from this is that if I had just stayed for around 15–20 years, recruited just one solid agent a year, and helped them do the same, in the 20th year, my company would be paying me over $20,000 per month. Big mistake, right? Well, I learned from it, and I am in a good place now. I want you to learn from it.

Find your spot, stay in your spot, and build. Take your time and build it right. I also applied that to the automotive industry. I have been in the automotive industry for 18 years, in only 2 dealerships. I know some guys that move every 6 months. I am not knocking these guys because I know a few of them that do well, but I recommend that you plant yourself and make your oil well pump oil. "Oil well" is a metaphor for your spot, which is going to make a lot of money.

In doing your research, look for a company that shares your values. Other than pay and benefits, most people say that they are attracted to a business because of meaningful work. If you own your own business, you can buy all the benefits you want by researching a company's core mission or your business's core mission. You are not only ensuring that they have clear goals, but also that they are ones that resonate with your interests and passions.

Set aside time to do necessary research. Find your spot, and make it pump oil for you and your family. Play the long game, take it slow, build one block at a time, and watch the magic. Be a student of the game.

Manager and Co-Workers

Wow, this is another good one. In the business world, you will get the chance to meet lots of different kinds of people. You have to remember though, when you are working with people that make 6 figures, there will be some arrogant S.O.B.s that know you will be around. Get used to it! Most of the time, they don't know what they are doing or saying. You are going to be top manager, so that's not going to be in your corner. Get used to it. In the automotive industry, I averaged over 20 cars a month, for 18 years. When I joined this car company, I and 8 others were on the sales floor. I was the only one that survived. Six of them got out of the automotive business, and one of them was offered a porter position. Over the years, different managers came through. Guess what? They would go to the porter to get car advice before they came to me. Now, this guy could sell a heater to an Eskimo. I'm not putting the porter down; he was a good guy, and being a porter is not a bad position.

It's just the disrespectful way in which they come across sometimes. Get used to it; when it comes to managers, it doesn't matter how long you have been in the business. They can make you think that you can't sell anything, if you let them. Stick to your sales that you have been successful with. You may have to change or make a few adjustments from time to time. I have had some good managers, but there are lots of them in the automotive industry that don't know what the hell they are doing. Get used to it.

Even though I have said all of that, most businesses and work places do have a good environment. You just have to know the personalities you are working with. Try to work with the manager that fits your personality. The same goes for your co-workers. You meet all kinds. Now, with the co-workers, you don't have to deal with them if you don't want to. I worked with a co-worker who was living with his mother, had a car that was no good (his cars were old), was in a bad relationship, and was not selling cars (8 cars on average, a month). He was walking around saying that somebody was jealous of him. On all levels, that is insane. You have those types; you can spot them a mile away, and you don't have to deal with them, unlike the managers. These types of people are insecure, and there are lots of them. You would think that if you have nothing going for you, then why would anyone be jealous of you? But you just need to know who you are dealing with. If anybody is in the type of situation that I describe, having nothing going for them, then you know there is a mental issue somewhere in their mind.

You also have co-workers trying to throw you off your game. That is a foolish strategy. I believe that it works against most people that try this. Think about it, use your time wisely, and think of things to make you better. I think it's wasted energy. I did not want to throw lots of negativity at you, but I want you to know what to look for. If you already have this knowledge, you will know how to navigate your way through the B.S., and nothing will hold you back. I want my mistakes and experience to help you pass all the bull, so that you can get to your destination easier. Remember, there is no free lunch. You have to put the work in, but by using this book, you can avoid lots of pitfalls.

To sum this part up, don't let managers and co-workers distract you from reaching your goals. You know why you are there. Go in every day on a mission. Always keep God first. Do the right thing, put your processes in place, and get your six figures.

Location

In business, location is everything. In doing your research, you want to be in the best location possible. I talked about how, when I was looking, I was willing to go in a 100-mile radius—north, south, east, or west—if the situation was the right one. Research different locations, and gather information about demographic and economic characteristics of the area you are interested in. Find out about other businesses in the area. Research your competitors, contact local councils, and consider the current and future needs of your business. The impact of location on business success is huge. The location of a person's business is one of the most important variables in determining potential success. A business that is located in a desirable area will benefit from the exposure and foot traffic of other neighborhood businesses. Moreover, the right setting for a corporation's headquarters can project a positive image that is more inviting for potential customers.

In regard to population demographics, find out if the majority of the human traffic in the area falls under your targeted customer base. For a fee, you can make use of location analysis tools. Grow and optimize (check the local chamber of commerce). That can give you information like traffic patterns and lifestyle data of those who come and go in the area. Such demographics include age, profession, and household income. By figuring out the nearby demographics, you will be able to know how well your product will sell in that vicinity.

Alternatively, you can save on the cost of a location analysis by looking at where your competition is. Fast food chains usually situate their business where there is human traffic. Seeing where your competitors are located gives you a good gauge of the feasibility of doing business in the area. It is then up to you to engineer your business to draw more customers to your location.

Make sure your shop front is visible from major roads and can easily be located. Visibility does not mean that you need to be right in the heart of the activity. Situating your business, such as a restaurant, a short distance away from major shopping malls will mean that you can enjoy the consumer traffic from the mall, without having to pay exorbitant rental costs. Amenities and accessibility is vital. Your business may be visible and offering a great product, but it is also important that your customers have easy access to it. A good location should have several nearby parking spots and gas stations to cater to those who arrive. It should also be as near as possible to bus stops or MRT stations, so that people can get to your location with ease.

Another consideration is the availability of infrastructure. Now, in a small business like mine, I just find somebody that is good with computers to help me out from time to time. Just keep it simple; you know that you need to be at a place that will support you financially. Do your research; I could say that is enough. The reason you should do good research is because you are going to be there for the long haul. It's going to be your home for a while. While you are doing your research, do some market research. Market research is further split into 2 varieties: primary and secondary. Primary research studies customers directly, whereas secondary research studies information that others have gathered about customers. Primary research might be telephone interviews or online polls with randomly selected members of the targeted group. You can also study your own sales records to gather primary research.

Secondary research might come from reports found on the website of various other organizations or blogs written about the industry. For your plan, you can use either type of research or a combination of both. Again, just keep it simple. If you noticed, I used the word *research* more than 12 times in this section. It's very important.

The Long Haul

This is the reason that you do good research. You want to be there (your spot) for the long haul. You will want customers to know where you are. You would be surprised how much repeat and referral business you can build up if customers know where you are. Learn to play the long game. Do you remember, earlier in this book, when I talked about a company (a good company) where I could have recruited 1 agent a year, for over 10, 15, or 20 years? I would have been in the 6-figure club. We want things to happen too fast. Now, don't get me wrong; you want to make sure something is happening. Your goals and plans should be made up of short gains with a long-haul ending.

Example: #1: If I research a company and see that I can make money, I put my plan in place. In this example, I am using the automotive industry. My plan would be to hustle for the first 2 years. As my customer base begins to build, I would then have repeat and referral business. This can work for any type of business.

Example #2: In the insurance industry, if you start your own agency, it is like any other business. I will learn the product really well, work real hard for the first 2 years, build my base, and ask for referrals from every customer I write up. As you can see, when you do your research, the rest is simple.

In building your business, just think of it as one brick at a time. Choose the right business, and choose the best location that you can. You may have heard this phrase: "It's a marathon, not a sprint." For some businesses today, however, the intent from day one really is a sprint. New companies are launched with the goals of first achieving lightning fast growth, and then being acquired by the highest bidder (some owners like to sell fast). For those whose business is an extension of themselves, not to mention a source of income for the long term, this mentality may seem alien, but it's most important to stay true to your goals. This may mean defining personal success as running a business you love, which also grows at a steady pace and brings steady profits.

There is nothing wrong with making your business your life's work. In fact, there are lots of highly successful entrepreneurs who do just that. Here are three suggestions to help you avoid short-term resist the grow and sell trends, and stick to your long-term vision so that you can run a business that makes you proud and supports you financially, year in and year out. How much do you need to grow each year in order to stay competitive? How much growth is too much, in that it would mean diluting the quality of your product, or acting contrary to your business mission? It can be difficult to forecast exactly how much you should plan to grow, but it's critical that you spend time considering these questions and setting some expectations. Beating your forecasted growth is a choice that usually requires clear investment in equipment, partners, and staff.

Be mindful about taking outside investments. I am not saying not to take outside investments. Be mindful more often than not; if an investor wants to write you a check, he or she is expecting rapid growth and a quick return resulting from the sale of your business or other capital events. He or she may also ask to own a sizable piece of the company. It may be tempting to take a large sum from someone who wants to give it to you, especially if you have big ideas, but sometimes turning away investment money can be the best choice for your business. If you are in need of capital to grow but do not want the conditions that might be associated with an investor, you might consider borrowing or some other means of getting capital to grow your business. I don't want to get too deep into this part of business, but remember that it does take time to build a successful business. Set your goals, put your plan in place, and go get it—it's yours!

Show Up

When I played sports, I showed up for every game. I came with my best—every game, every minute, every hour, and every second. Now, I know, some days you just don't feel like it. Those are the days where you really have to talk to yourself, and recommit to your plans and goals. On those days, you will have to dig deep and push yourself; however, you should not have too many of those days. I remember one game when I was playing post level baseball every year when I was in Germany. I was the starting shortstop. The coach told me early on that I needed to play third base. Our starting third baseman was out with an injury. It was during tournament time, and we had already went to several army posts and had kicked butt. The competition would only get better. Well, I guess I put too much thought into it. The other team rocked me. That ball looked like BBs coming down that third baseline.

That was a tough day for me. They were singing "We Will Rock You" as they were doing it. Wow, I will never forget that day. That was a day where I had to dig deep. My position was not the only one getting rocked. So, what did I do? We were in the game, so there was no turning back. Being one of the captains on the team, I sent a sign to the coach to call time-out, and to have a meeting on the mound while everyone was on the field, not in the dugout. You know how those meetings go; we get in each other's butts. We had to readjust our thinking and get it done.

Again, some days will be tough. Have some type of mental or physical mechanism or routine to do at that time, and keep it simple. When I say *show up*, I mean *make something happen*. You make a difference when you show up anywhere. Why is showing up necessary to be successful in business? Success in business is about setting goals and achieving them; and the secret, as many people will agree, is to put in the work. All successful people put in the work. I have heard some people say that if you want to be successful in business, put work at the top of your goals list. If you really show up each day, you will automatically do the other two things that lead to success in business: You will improve yourself, and you will persist.

Showing up (hard work) and success go hand in hand, because nothing is offered on a silver platter, which means that people have to keep trying to succeed. Rupert Murdoch says, *"It's all hard work. Nothing comes easy."* Martha Stewart says, *"I'm a real hard worker. I work, work, and work, all the time. Make your work your recreation."* Bill Gates is a hard worker. Even after he was a multi-millionaire, he worked most nights until 10 pm. Oprah Winfrey is a hard worker. She says, *"I would never see daylight. I would come into work at 5:30 am, when it's dark, and leave between 7 and 8 pm, when it's dark. I am a hard worker."* Over the years, I have gone through many days and even weeks without much sleep, just because I wanted to grow my business and achieve success.

I have to admit, at times, you say to yourself: "Am I the only one working this hard?" There is a myth that it comes easy to some people. You turn on the TV, and no one is working hard. A comedian like Kevin Hart stands up on stage and tells a few jokes. What's hard about that? But even Kevin Hart says, *"Everybody wants to be famous, but no one wants to do the work."* I live by that. You grind hard so that you can play harder. You show up, and at the end of the day, it will eventually pay off. It could be in a year, 2 years, or 5 years, but it will pay off. Show up, and make a difference in your family's financial life. Put the work in, and watch the magic.

Let Them Know What You Bring to the Table

This is another good one. I went to an interview at an insurance company. It's a big company, and it's hard to become a part of them. I was asked why they should make me a part of their company...Wow. Most people would not have been prepared for that question, but I was. I said, "Mr. Jones, I'm glad you asked that question." You see, I had made some condensed charts that showed a big improvement on the company's bottom line. I showed him my production flow chart. I always keep my average sales and contacts, meaning that I know how many people to see to make a deal or sale. I asked him what the average number was at the end of the month there. Then I told him and showed him how I would add 20 sales to their bottom line. And I did not just tell him—I showed him. I also told him that I am a team player and that they would be adding a quality person to their team. Most of the people that work there come from rich families, but that didn't bother me.

One thing I know is that hard work beats talent. Unfortunately, many talented people don't achieve as much success as they could, because they sit back and rely on their talent, and never learned to work hard. All people tend to underestimate work, and overestimate talent. That's what happened to Michael Jordan when he first started playing basketball. He had the talent, but he was not putting in the work, and his coach actually cut him from the high school basketball team. He said that he was very disappointed. He started working on his game the day after he got cut, and that hard work made him the greatest basketball player of all time. So I would say that the real gift is not talent; it's the ability to work hard.

Work wins over smarts. Some individuals argue that an individual doesn't need to be hard working to be successful. In fact, many successful people are not the smartest; they just work the hardest. Therefore, it is hard work and not smart work that breeds success. As a result, they were able to stand out amongst the crowd. Thomas Stanley studied hundreds of millionaires, and he discovered that most millionaires were not "A" students in school or college. They did not score high on tests, and teachers did not think they would ever be successful, but they did succeed because they worked hard. You can still succeed as long as you work hard.

Hardworking people try to find ways of solving some of the setbacks instead of giving up. More so, they put in more effort, even when it looks like they are not winning. So, the bottom line is, whether you are smart or not, and whether you are talented or not, you should just keep working. Hard work is the only key to achieving; it teaches us discipline, dedication, and determination. Hard work is definitely more important because it is only through hard work that we can achieve the goals of our life. Hard work is challenging, painful, and uncomfortable, but it's the only way to the top. In fact, a major key to success is to learn to enjoy challenging work, and to enjoy working hard at it. For most people, work is hard enough without pushing even harder.

Hard work is the single greatest competitive advantage. Nobody is great without work. Hard work is always the baseline of great achievements. Nothing spectacular comes without it. Getting organized is hard work. Setting goals, making plans to achieve them, and staying on track is hard work. Very few have ever failed with the hard work approach when it comes to making it in life. You may rise slowly, but you will rise.

There are no shortcuts to lasting success. Many will do what's easiest and avoid hard work, and that's precisely why you should do the opposite. Lasting success can only be achieved if you put in the work. Jim Rohn says, *"Don't wish it were easier; wish you were better."*

"So, this is what I bring to the table. If you hire me, your whole team will function better. I have an awesome system that I work by." Know your worth, and don't let anyone take it from you. Don't let anyone bring you down. I got the position, and in one month, I led the team in sales!

Chapter 7

Earn the Business

People Don't Like to Be Sold

Customers, nowadays, love to feel like they made a smart purchase. Your job is to sell to them but also to make them feel like they have made an intelligent decision. In the old days, you would sell to a customer, tell them anything, and they knew you were not being upfront with them, but they had no way to prove it. Now, we have the internet. You can research anything.

When a customer comes to your place of business, they already know what to expect, and they know prices. You have to be able to deal with the new type of customer. People don't like to be sold to, but they love to buy. The power of that statement is all the insight into the selling process. For the last 20 years, salespeople have been taught how to sell, and I am saying to you that this is the least powerful way of completing a transaction. Salespeople learn technique, salespeople learn closes, and salespeople learn systems of selling, but none of them are more powerful than someone wanting to buy. In fact, all of them are useless if someone does not want to buy, is afraid to buy, or do not like the person he or she is buying from.

Rather than selling, take a look at buying. Would you rather know how to sell, or would you rather know why people buy? The answer is that we want to know why people buy. You can argue that relationship building, questioning skills, networking, and presentation skills are all part of the selling process, and I agree; but I stand firm that *buying motives are a million times more powerful than selling skills.* A buying motive may have to do with how much money one may have, or it may be about how much of a risk one has to take to make the purchase. It might be about whether it will work when they get home. It might be about whether it will increase productivity in their company.

Think of your buying motives. Why do you buy? You decide that you need or want something. Then you justify the need or the want, and you literally search for it. You set out on a Saturday afternoon to spend money. You may go shopping, or you may go directly to the establishment that has what you want. Either way, your motive is clear ownership, as soon as possible. If your buying motive is strong enough, your spouse, children, parents, and especially salespeople, can't keep you from getting what you want.

Whatever it is, by the end of the day, you are going to make a heroic effort to own it. And, *buy* the way (not *by* the way), that need is defined as an emotion; it has nothing to do with logic. One of the primary motives for buying is an emotional one; and in the emotional state, people will overpay to get what they want.

Customers will buy emotionally, and justify it. Here is the problem. Most salespeople don't know how to let the sale flow so that it can happen. Just listen! I define it as the head being attached to the wallet. If I pull on the heartstrings, the wallet will pop out of the back pocket, and the only thing that can stop it is logic. You ask then why they buy. It never ceases to amaze me how complex selling situations become because they are sales trainer driven rather than customer driven.

For many of you, this is a brand new thought, and as with all brand new thoughts, there is a hesitancy based on a lack of experience or success. My two words of advice are: TRY IT! Remember, customers don't like to be sold to. They want to feel like they are in control. I would say that maybe 2 out of 100 will come in and say, "Sell me on this." As a sales professional, you have to learn how to make them feel in control, but you are really in control. You do that by listening for those hot buttons. Whatever industry you are in, have hot buttons. For example, in the car industry, it could be safety, performance, or style... I could go on and on. In real estate, it could be something else. Whatever it is, get them emotionally attached, and earn the business.

Let Them Know That You Are with Them

I can remember, during my time as a sales professional, the times where I told the customer that I was on their side, and I really meant that. This can sound really corny, so you have to be genuine when you say it. Most people can spot a phony miles away, so just be real. If you are not genuine, don't say it. You can have the most efficient experience in the industry, but if customers don't feel like you care about them, they will not stay loyal. Here's how the people who interact with customers can consistently show they care. Most organizations find it easier to teach sales professionals the hard skills that they need in order to do the job well, than to improve the soft skills, but it's the soft signs of caring, empathy, listening, and concern that matter most to the customer's experience.

Your best strategy is to teach your sales professional what caring about customers looks like in action. When they see how good it feels to care, and how good caring is for business, you will receive your team's total buy-in and continued participation. As business gets more complicated by technology, it's often the simple things that can make customers feel great. Give customers your full attention by taking eyes and ears off all the distractions around you when they talk. I can tell you how many times I have seen sales professionals answer a sales call with a customer sitting right in front of them. Please don't do this. Leaders need to set the example here, and maybe call out the salesperson.

The Book on Sales

Offer to help, but don't hover. If customers visit you, acknowledge them quickly, if not immediately, and offer help. Of course, much more business happens online and on the phone these days. So when customers are online, offer a chat session, but don't have chat box offers popping up over and over. On the phone, end every conversation with one more offer to help, in case the customer thinks of something else. Make it personal. Most frontline sales professionals probably learned a long time ago to address customers by name, to make the experience more personal.

That still holds true, but adding a memory—perhaps referring to a past experience or personal information that the customer shared at another time—shows you care about the customer, not just the transaction. Most databases leave room for notes. Encourage sales professionals to make short notes that they and colleagues can use as references to past conversations that can and should be mentioned again. I remember the time when a new customer came to my place of business. He was driving a black SUV Volvo. He told me his story, and I listened. He and his family were living in Macon, GA, but he worked in Ohio. He was flying to Ohio every Monday morning. I gave him what he needed to make a buying decision. He told me he would be back. He showed up about 8 months later. I remembered the black Volvo SUV. He got out of the vehicle, and I went up to him and said, "John, how are you? Are you still flying to Ohio? Man, we're so impressed to have earned your business." He told all the managers how he was so satisfied with me.

Show respect. Surely, sales professionals who deal with customers know to be respectful. There are extra steps you can take to show respect, beyond listening closely, speaking kindly, and using a kind tone. Show customers respect by recognizing something they have done. It can be as simple as complimenting them on a choice they made during the order, or if they reveal any accomplishments, perhaps mentioning a work promotion, a 5k finish, or a child's college graduation during the rapport building conversations. Compliment

74

them on the effort it took to achieve that, and note it in their account so that you can follow up sometime down the road. It's nearly impossible to set a caring tone when talking negatively about your job, competitors, customers, the industry, weather, or whatever. A negative culture is not a caring one. When you see the good, look for the good and expect the good; you will find the good, and the good will find you. Find a way to let them know that you have their back, and mean it.

Let Them Feel the Genuine Attitude

This one can be tricky. This is a learned skill. I have met some people that are born with it, but I don't know many people that are straight shooters. I also know some people that I wouldn't deal with at all. Most customers can tell the difference. So 95% of the time, the customer has already figured you out. Work on this.

Being genuine and sincere means being honest and straight forward without any pretense, misrepresentation, or deceit. Being a more genuine person can refer to how you interact with others, but ultimately, sincerity must begin within yourself. Learning to recognize your thoughts and feelings can help you become a more genuine person, which in turn can help you become more sincere in your dealings with others.

Use sincere body language. Body language can convey a great deal about your attitude, and it can easily reveal sincerity (or lack thereof). When you interact with others, try to be mindful of your posture, mannerisms, and behavior. Make steady eye contact, but don't stare. Look away every now and then, and don't forget to blink. Maintain a relaxed posture, but keep your body slightly poised. You can do this by very slightly leaning toward the person you are talking to, or reaching out/gesturing toward that person. Don't try to change your body language to reflect sincerity. If you are sincere, your body language will naturally show it.

Be an active listener. One easy way to show sincerity to others is by being an active listener. As someone speaks to you, keep an open mind about what someone is saying. Practicing active listening skills shows others that you are taking a sincere interest in what they have to say, and that you genuinely want to know more about the thoughts and feelings of others.

Face the person you are talking to. When you have a genuine reaction to what someone else is saying, your facial cues will give that reaction away. You will raise your eyebrows, your eyes may widen, and your mouth will reveal your emotional reactions. Facing someone will let them see your reactions, and it will convey to them that you are engaged and interested.

Ask open-ended questions to allow the other person to elaborate. For example, don't just ask, "Did you like living there?" This type of question will elicit a yes response. Instead, you can ask something like, "Wow, I have never been there before. What was it like for you? What are some memories you have of living there?" This shows your engagement and your curiosity. Reflect on what has been said by the other person before giving your response. Your conversational partner may be thinking of how to phrase something, or simply leaving a pause in the conversation for dramatic effect. If you rush to say whatever is on your mind, it will not convey a sincere conversational interest in that person's thoughts and opinions.

Understand another person's point of view. If you refuse to consider why another person thinks/feels the way they do, you will not be able to have a sincere conversation with that person. Understanding someone else's point of view does not necessarily mean abandoning your own perspective. Rather, you should try to understand what motivates others, and what life experiences may have shaped another person's point of view. Once you are capable of seeing the world through someone else's eyes, you will develop a more sincere understanding of who that person is, and what made him the way he is.

Instead of criticizing someone else's musical tastes, for example, try to understand what about that music might be appealing. Perhaps the lyrics speak to the other person, or perhaps the loud bass lines of a dance song allows someone who is normally shy to break out of their shell and make moves on the dance floor. Just be genuine and sincere. If you can't do that, find something else to do. I hate to say it like that, but if you can't be straight with a customer, they will soon find you out anyway.

I Will Be Here

Have you ever went to a furniture store, bought furniture, and had to go back with a problem, but the person you were dealing with was gone? Or bought a vehicle, and the salesperson was gone when you went back with a question? I can answer that: Yes. This is why, earlier in this book, I told you to do your research. You want to find the right place, because you will be there for the long haul.

People want to know if you're going to be there for them. I remember a time when a husband, wife, and daughter came into the dealership. I greeted them. The family was from Florida. The daughter was up here going to Mercer University. After listening to the family, I knew what their concerns were, especially the father's. I told the husband and wife that if their daughter had problems (car problems), she wouldn't have to call them in Florida, and if she did, they could just call me, and I would take care of the problem. *"Sir, you go back to Florida with no worries. I will be your car agent."* Wow, they were so impressed that they got their other daughter, who was coming to Mercer University next, a vehicle too. When customers make a big purchase, they are depending on you. Over the years, that happens so many times. Let them know that you will be there.

Adopting the following phrases in your customer support vocabulary will allow you to quickly improve how you deliver support. What about this one: "I don't know, but I will find out for you"—and there's nothing wrong with that. In a customer service survey, American Express asked respondents which common customer service phrases annoyed them most. Here it is: "We are unable to answer your question. Please call xxx-xxx-xxxx to speak to a representative from our team." When you have a problem, you don't want to hear that. I would rather have someone, who I can depend on, tell me that they will find out for me.

Despite how or why a situation happened, customers want to know you care. They want to know that you care about their feelings, can relate, and that your goal is to solve their problems. The way your service skills handle issue resolution is crucial to your business, reputation, client retention, and more.

Customers want to be treated in such a manner that is consistent with their own values. Here are some effective ways to show your customers empathy so that they know you care. Listen intently to the customer, and do not talk over them. Don't just hear them; make the effort to understand what they are saying, and do not interrupt them. They want to feel heard, not rushed or overlooked. Consider how you would feel in their shoes.

Recap the issue or complaint before solving it. By recapping the issue with the customer, you reinforce that you are paying attention, not just breathing on the other end of the phone line. This also proves that you are leveling with them and understand. Use phrases like "thank you" and "I'm very sorry!" Phrases like these create calm, comfort, and confidence within the customer. These phrases are also very polite, and that shows the customer that you respect them.

Relate to their plan or issue. Don't leave your humanity at the door; relate to the customer's issue by anticipating how you would feel in their situation. Seeing things from their perspective will prove your thoughtfulness and consideration. Stay professional. Even if the customer becomes angry or inappropriate, you must remain calm and respectful. Maintaining this tone usually calms down an angered customer, but even if it does not, remember that you are representing yourself and your business during every customer engagement—so represent well!

Just be there for them, and let them know that you will be there!

What Do I Need to Do?

This is a phrase used when you are deep in negotiation. You have done all the right things, and now you want to earn the business. In so many ways, you have done a lot already, if you have taken the professional steps I talked about in the earlier chapters. Please, at this time, after the question, shut up and listen. They will tell you what to do to earn the business. When it comes to professional selling, there is one thing that is always true: Somebody gets sold on something, whether you sell your customer on why they should buy your product today, or they sell you on why they are not buying today. What is it going to be? Are you going to sell to your customer, or are they going to sell you on one of their reasons for not buying now?

This is one thing to ask yourself every time you are with a customer, and it is probably one of the most important things a sales professional should know. Who is getting sold on something—you or them? Sometimes they will try to turn it around on you, but remember that you are the sales professional. When they say, "I am just browsing," of course, they are at your place of business to check things out; and nothing will happen until they meet a sales professional, but not just any salesperson—it must be a professional. They won't tell you that they are there to make a purchase; they will tell you that they are just browsing and will be buying in the future, but if you are a true professional, you will sell them your product today, or at least in the near future. Just looking or just browsing is the first line of defense against the sales professional. You can accept it or you can sell them your product—you decide. Top sales professionals understand that.

Bad mouthing your competitors will hurt more than help. Don't let yourself get caught in the trap of bad mouthing your competing sales professionals, at other locations that are selling the same product as you, because it will do more harm than good. You don't know what they are thinking, and you might even be insulting them without knowing it. Show them why your place of business is the best place to buy the product they are looking for. When I say product, it could be insurance, automotive, real estate, etc. I have seen many sales lost after a salesman talked trash about another company or brand.

Use the selling system that you were trained to use to sell your product, and don't start thinking that you know a better way. This is the quickest way to see your sales drop. When you start leaving things out and short cutting the system, you could be shooting yourself in the foot. Professional sales training systems were designed to work throughout your business and to be consistent. One step is made to work with the next. I will guarantee that you will lose sales when you start thinking that you know better, or you start short cutting the system.

This is one of the things a sales professional should know but often forgets. Stay with the basics, and you will sell more products than you will ever believe. Here is another biggie: Stop thinking that the price is the only thing that will close the sale, because that is not the case. Almost everyone is willing to pay more when they see the value in something. Start working your customer harder, and provide more value. Show them what's in it for them. The thing a sales professional should know and never forget is that whether they are a newbie or a veteran, it's not always about price. It doesn't matter what you are selling.

What about this one: "I will be back." I don't believe in "be backs". This is why, earlier in this book, I have the road map to the sale. A high percentage of your "be backs" won't be back. Knowing that you have taken no short cuts, and that you have taken the proper steps, and they say, "Well, I will be back," this is when you want to know and ask, "What do I need to do to earn your business?"

It's All About the Customer

I don't know if you have noticed, but there are customer surveys, google reviews, and all kinds of customer reviews out there. So everything is customer based these days. Measuring your sales process has to be customer based. You have to learn how to sell and how to satisfy the customer at the same time. Some people can't do this, but it's not hard.

Not only is customer service a deeper field than those outside, it's evolving at an unprecedented pace. Along with the marketplace, customer attitudes and business responses have shifted. Chat and messaging are here to stay. Millennials have spending power and prefer different methods of communication, and we have barely scratched the surface where empowered customer support is concerned.

Do you know the cost of bad service? More than half of Americans have scrapped a planned purchase or transaction because of bad service. Thirty-three percent of Americans say that they will consider switching companies after just one single instance of poor service. U.S. companies lose more than $62 billion annually due to poor customer service. WOW!

So, like I said, it's all about the customer. Now that we know that, here are some things we can do. Excellent customer service creates loyal customers for life. Customers are willing to refer your business to friends, family, and colleagues, providing this type of excellent customer service starts with a genuine desire to delight your customers; but you also have to think beyond selling your products or services. You need to consider the cumulative experience that your customers have when they visit your place of business or your website, as well as what they think and feel, and what you can do to make it better. In order to provide good customer service, you need to know what you are selling, inside and out. Make sure you know how your products and services work. Be aware of the most common questions customers ask, and know how to articulate the answers that will leave them satisfied.

Be friendly. As they say, customer service starts with a smile. When you are in a face-to-face situation, a warm greeting should be the first thing your customers hear when they ask for help. Even when handling customer service requests via telephone, a smile can come through in your voice, so make sure you are ready to be friendly.

Say thank you. Gratitude is memorable, and it can remind your customer why they shopped at your place of business or hired your company. Regardless of the type of business you have, saying thank you after every transaction is one of the easiest ways to start a habit of good customer service. If you have employees that work for you, it's important to make sure that all of them—not just your customer service representatives—understand the way they should talk to, interact with, and problem solve for customers. Provide employee training that gives your staff the tools they need to carry good customer service through the entire customer experience.

Show respect. Customer service can often involve emotions, so it's important to make sure that you and others that you have handling your customer service tasks are always courteous and respectful. Never let your own emotions overtake your desire to see your customers walk away happy.

Listen. Listening is one of the simplest secrets of customer service. Listening means hearing what your customers are communicating nonverbally. Watch for signs that they are displeased, while listening to what they say to you directly.

Be responsive. To a customer who is trying to get help, resolve an issue, or find out more about what you are selling, there may be nothing worse than nonresponsiveness. It's important to respond quickly to all inquiries, even if it is only to say that you are looking into the issue and will be in touch. Some responses are always better than none, so that the customer does not feel ignored.

Have you heard that the customer is always right? Remember, it's all about the customers. The customer pays your bills, and they don't mind paying your bills, if you treat them right.

–

Chapter 8

The Review

In this chapter, we will go over the steps and principles that we talked about in earlier chapters. The reason we are going back over these chapters is because they are very important. When you use them, you will see why. I talked about the fundamentals. The fundamentals are the basics. Fundamentals of sales are about mastering the mindset, which allows a professional salesperson to learn any skills, methodology, tools, and buying processes so that they are relevant, transparent, and more helpful to the buyer than their website is.

There was a recent conversation happening among sales leaders, managers, and representatives, around the question, "Does mastering the fundamentals lead to improved sales performance?" It is no surprise that the answer is, "Yes, of course it does." Sales fundamentals come down to supportive beliefs. We all grow up with a set of personal beliefs. How we were raised to behave, and what we were taught to think, influences and shapes our belief system. What your internal voice tells you will influence your sales behaviors, and will either support or hinder your success. Some beliefs will limit or encourage a strong self-image and the relationship with prospects. Others will influence buying decisions, size of deals, and how managers/executives manage people and processes.

The ability to control your emotions is a must. Being emotionally involved in a sale takes you out of the present. You think about the future or the next step. You are not in the present moment, and you are not hearing what your customers are actually saying, including the tone and inflection of their voices. You are losing your objectivity and your ability to offer insight and develop happy ears that tell you what you want to hear (they are ready to buy!). This will inhibit your ability to listen and ask questions with ease. You will also likely get frustrated and try to move things along, only to push away prospects with your tactics.

Be comfortable discussing money. When your customer pushes back because you are too expensive, you are likely to agree with them. Instead of helping a customer focus on the price, let them know the different price and cost. I would say, "You can get a cheaper product, but it will cost you more in the long run. Let me give you an example. I had a customer that was looking at a vehicle. He wanted to compare prices with a vehicle at another location. I knew the company he was talking about, and I asked him if he was worried about price or cost. My vehicle is priced a little more than the other one you are looking at, but the other vehicle will cost you more."

I knew that the other company didn't condition their vehicles at all; they just buy them from the auction and put them on the lot. My company buys them, runs them through the shop, and then puts them on the lot. I knew I had the better product. This is why you need to know your competition. He went with the other company, and about 3 months later, this same guy came back into the dealership. He asked whether I was still there, and someone showed him where I was. He said, "I tried everything I could, but everything you told me was true." The motor had gone bad about 3 months after getting the car. He put money in it to try to keep it running, but it was costing him too much. I helped him out and got him out of that situation.

Let your customer know that there are prices and costs. You can get a cheaper product, but it will cost you more. You must have the ability to handle rejections that stem from your own self-image. When you are comfortable with who you are and the values that you bring, you can understand that it's not you that's rejected but just your offer to help. When rejection no longer inhibits you, you will be able to ask the appropriate thought provoking questions, and become a thought leader and trusted advisor in your prospect's/client's mind.

Some people ask whether fundamentals are only for new people, and the answer is a big NO! I have worked with veteran salespeople and new salespeople alike, and they struggle with these same fundamentals. Just because you have been selling for 20 years, it doesn't mean you have mastered these fundamentals. In fact, research from the objective management group of over a million salespeople, across the globe and in all industries, shows that only 6% have mastered the fundamentals and skills of sales, whereas 20% do okay but could improve. Of the remaining 74%, 25% of them should not be in sales at all—not only do they not have the fundamentals and skills, they are not coachable or trainable either. That leaves 49% that could improve with work, because they are trainable and coachable.

To me, fundamentals are just the basics. Get training, and do what you should do without missing steps in your sales process. STICK WITH THE FUNDAMENTALS.

Getting Comfortable

Getting comfortable can be hard sometimes for new sales professionals, and I have also seen older sales professionals with this problem. It's an easy fix. Of all the things an entrepreneur can be afraid of, there aren't many that rank higher than the fear of selling.

While some believe that the fear of failure is the biggest barrier to success, you should not be afraid to fail. Some just fear interacting with customers. I was trained to take it head on. When I'm walking up to a customer that seems intimidating, I say to myself, "Good." I want to notice it, confront it, and then overcome it. If you do this, you will soon overcome it all together. Here are a few tips:

1. Know the source of your fear. This one reminds me that it's necessary to first know what you're afraid of. Most often, the fear of selling comes in several forms. We worry about not being liked, or of being perceived as pushy. We (secretly) worry that our product or service might not perform as we say, and we struggle with the idea of rejection. Knowing the source of your fear (sometimes it can be a combination) is an important part of overcoming your fears of selling.

2. Take action to address the source. In this way, you are taking action to overcome your fear. In some cases, this might mean that you improve your product or service (use customer feedback for this), or you can find ways to share your product or service in a way that feels more authentic and natural to you. You can also find ways to bounce back after rejection—which is easier to do, by the way, if you don't take anything personally.

3. Find enthusiasm for what you offer. One of the best techniques I have used to overcome my fear of selling has been to tap into my passion and enthusiasm for what I am offering. I make a list of all the really wonderful benefits and successful outcomes of past customers. I put the list nearby so that I can see it every day. This will help your confidence sky rocket.

4. Shift your perspective. How does it feel to think of yourself as sharing information about what you do? Or showing benefits or sharing your passion? If you feel uncomfortable or anxious about selling, find a way to shift your perspective to one of sharing information rather than convincing someone to buy.

5. Be smart. Very often, people tend to tackle projects much larger than they can comfortably handle. When you want to overcome the fear of selling, start small. Maybe you will share your new business with a few trusted friends first, and then gradually find ways to expand your sharing to include a larger circle. The most

successful businesspeople are those who interact with others in an authentic, passionate way; so find a way that feels comfortable, and stay with it.

6. Keep track of your success. Keep a success journal nearby, and record your achievements in it each day. This will help you to stay aware of just how much you do right. We sometimes forget this.

7. Have fun with it. Rather than approaching this from a heavy "have-to-but-doesn't-feel-good" perspective, find a fun and interesting way to share your knowledge or passion. Some of my customers have thrown parties. I offered free giveaways, donated products and services to charities, and all of these were easy, fun, and income generating. What would be fun for you?

8. Stay focused on your desired outcome. Most people take action and reach their goals because they stay focused on the benefits of doing so. Sometimes reminding yourself what you want and why you are doing this can help you stay motivated.

9. Detach from how the outcome shows up. Very often, we get really attached to making the sale or having a situation turn out a certain way. Instead, why not focus on efforts? "I will give a great, enthusiastic and passionate presentation, rather than concentrate on the outcome." They will buy an x number of this very often. If you stay focused on the effort, and are doing a great job, the outcome will turn out better than ever imagined.

10. Keep practicing. Like in any other business, selling gets easier the more you do it. So, get out there, start smart, and keep practicing. Take it head on, and watch the magic.

Develop a Plan

I wanted the book to be a really successful tool for your professional career. This is why I am reviewing some of the things we went over in earlier chapters. Finding a good plan, and sticking to it, is very important. Make sure that it's a plan of action. A well-thought-out sales professional development plan provides your sales career with opportunities and clear direction on how to increase your skills and advance your career, with a more expanded skill set. You will have more tools to help your business forge ahead. It's a win-win for you.

Before you set objectives for a sales professional development plan, try to align your development needs with your company. Once you have identified your objectives, you can identify the necessary skills, knowledge, and competencies that support those goals. I remember when I was with a slow-paced company. After about 3 years, the company wanted to become a fast-paced company. So my objectives changed from slow-paced to fast-paced. Therefore, my plans changed.

Now that you know what the objectives are, it's time to develop your plan accordingly. Your plan doesn't have to be expensive, but make sure that you keep self training in it. Once you have identified some specific learning opportunities, create a plan with specific and timely goals. It's much more difficult to measure your progress when the objective is vague, overly broad, or you don't have a deadline. Next, what is it going to take to put your plan into action? Is there any prep work needed to be done?

To develop your plan, it is helpful to identify your priorities and develop a realistic action plan. Choose the top five, and turn them into goal statements. Developing an action plan can help change makers turn their visions into reality, and increase efficiency and accountability within yourself and your organization. An action plan describes the way you will meet the objective, through detailed action steps that describe how and when these steps will be taken. This section provides a guide for developing and utilizing your action plan.

What goes in an action plan? In some ways, an action plan is a heroic act. It helps us turn our dreams into a reality. An action plan is a way to make sure that your vision is concrete. It describes the way you will use its strategies to meet its objectives. An action plan consists of a number of action steps or changes to be brought about in your professional business. Why should you develop an action plan? There is an inspirational saying: People don't plan to fail; instead, they fail to plan. Because you certainly don't want to fail, it makes sense to take all of the steps necessary to ensure success, including developing an action plan.

There are lots of good reasons to work out the details of your sales professional work in an action plan, including: to lend credibility to your business, which shows that you and your company are well organized and dedicated to getting things done; to make sure you don't overlook any of the details; to understand what is and isn't possible for your business to do; for efficiency, in order to save time, energy, and resources in the long run; and for accountability, to increase the chances that you will do what needs to be done. Your plan should have a vision and a mission, and objectives and strategies. Develop an action plan composed of action steps that address all proposed changes. The plan should be complete, clear, and current. Additionally, the action plan should include information and ideas that you have already gathered while brainstorming about your objectives and your strategies. What are the steps you must take to carry out your objectives while still fulfilling your vision and mission?

Now it's time to put all of the components together (vision, mission, objectives, and strategies). While the plan might address general goals that you want to see accomplished, the action steps will help you determine the specific actions you will take to help make your vision become a reality. Get your action plan in place, and watch the magic.

Find Your Spot

We have always heard that location is everything. It's very important. Being in a high traffic area means that the probability is that you will have more customers coming to your place of business.

Finding your spot is a little more than just location. Finding your spot can be the industry you choose (where you are your own independent company). You can choose a company to work for. We talk about doing your research because you will want to be there for the long haul. We spend a large part of our adult life at work, and it can significantly affect our well-being, both physically and mentally. This is why choosing a career is something that you should not take lightly. It's important to explore all the options available to you before you make a final decision, as this will help ensure your future professional happiness. Don't have an accidental life or career. Often, more planning goes into a summer vacation than a 40-year career or a 90-year life. Spend purposeful time on your career.

In finding your spot, you also want it to be a good environment. Whether you are applying for anything from an auditing job to a sales job, good communication within the workplace is essential for fostering a positive work environment. Everything is not going to be perfect, but you want to get as close to perfect as you can. Chances are, if employees communicate well with each other, and managers communicate well with the employees, the workplace will be more positive and productive.

Having fun is one way of effectively managing and improving employees' emotions. When you find your spot in a company, these are the type of managers you are looking for. It has also been proven to improve teamwork, build trusting relationships, and help you to stay at a location longer. As humans, we are social creatures that need a little fun in order to cope with the daily stressors that we face. When you pull up to your regular parking space at work, what's the first thought that crosses your mind as you shut the car door behind you and make your way to your office? Is the stress already starting to build? Is there a little lump of dread growing in your stomach? Do you get a little rush of happiness at the thought of the fun you are about to have? The last scenario is unfortunately not the norm at most companies, which probably hurts your performance. This is why finding your spot is so important, or should I say finding your best spot?

This is why being in a good environment is beneficial for business. Too often, business owners and managers think that all work and no play is the best way to maximize productivity. It's a good thing that researches don't automatically prescribe to this nation. Studies over the last 20 years have revealed that when workplaces make fun a factor, they create happier employees. Employees that feel more satisfied and happy are better at their jobs.

This is the type of environment you want to be in. Workplace fun has been linked to enhanced motivation, increased productivity, reduced stress, higher job satisfaction, and improved task performance. Why would you not want to be in a workplace like that? Remember to get as close to perfect as you can, but there is no perfect workplace. At the end of the day, it's all about one thing: the company culture that you want to create, and more importantly, that you want to work in. If your spot is your company, take time to celebrate wins. Create milestones that your whole company can celebrate together. Better yet, start an initiative to set aside a small percentage of the profits for your employee parties and events. Employees will work harder when they know that they will be rewarded and acknowledged for their contributions.

Either way you go at it (company owner or working for a company), find the best spot, or make the best spot, and watch the magic.

Set Goals

There is a reason that I have 2 chapters on goal setting. Goal setting is very important. Writing them down is very important. Goal setting is an important method for deciding what you want to achieve in your life, as well as for separating what's important from what's irrelevant or a distraction, and for building your self-confidence, based on the successful achievement of goals.

Plan to live your life your way. Many people feel as if they are adrift in this world. They work hard, but they don't seem to get anywhere worthwhile. How do you set a goal? First, consider what you want to achieve, and then commit to it. Set smart (specifically measureable, attainable, relevant, and time-bound) goals that motivate you, and write them down to make them feel tangible. Then plan the steps you must take to realize your goal, and cross off each one as you work through them.

Goal setting is a powerful process for thinking about your ideal future and for motivating yourself to turn your vision of this future into reality. The process of setting goals helps you choose where you want to go in life. By knowing precisely what you want to achieve, you know where you have to concentrate your efforts. You will also quickly spot the distractions that can so easily lead you astray.

Why set goals? Top level athletes, successful business people, and achievers in all fields, all set goals. Setting goals gives you long-term vision and short-term motivation. It focuses your acquisitions of knowledge, and helps you to organize your time and your resources so that you can make the most of your life. By setting sharp and clearly defined goals, you can measure and take pride in the achievement of those goals, and you will see forward progress in what might previously have seemed a long pointless grind. You also raise your self-confidence as you recognize your own ability and competence in achieving the goals that you have set.

Start setting personal goals. You set your goals on a number of levels. First, you create your big picture of what you want to do with your life (or over say the next ten years), and identify the large-scale goals that you want to achieve. Then you break these down into smaller and smaller targets that you must hit to reach your lifetime goals. Finally, once you have your plan, you start working on it to achieve these goals. This is why we start the process of setting goals by looking at your lifetime goals. Then we work down to the things that you can do in the next 5 years, then next year, next month, next week, or today, to start moving toward them.

To give a broad, balanced coverage of all important areas of your life, try to set goals in some of the following areas:

Career: What level do you want to reach in your career, or what do you want to achieve?

Financial: How much do you want to earn, and by what stage? How is this related to your career goals? Education: Is there any knowledge you want to acquire in particular? What information and skills will you need to have in order to achieve other goals?

Family: Do you want to be a parent? If so, how are you going to be a good parent? Family is very important.

Attitude: Is any part of your mindset holding you back? Is there any part of the way that you behave that upsets you? (If so, set a goal to improve your behavior, or find a solution to the problem.).
Physical: Are there any athletic goals that you want to achieve, or do you want good health deep into old age?

What steps are you going to take to achieve this?

Pleasure: How do you want to enjoy yourself? You should ensure that some of your life is for you. Spend some time brainstorming these things, and then select one or more goals in each category that best reflects what you want to do. Be serious; it's your future—set clear goals, and watch the magic!

Be Genuine and Earn the Business

How many times have you been sold to, with that sinking feeling that the seller could care less about your goals, wants, or needs, and you were hoping that you were not being dumped? It's a pretty icky feeling, and chances are that we have all been there at least once. I have been thinking a lot about how salespeople, including myself, could be more genuine to really make a difference. I come from the school of thought that those in the dynamic world of sales should do everything in their power to disprove the negative stereotypes that are often attributed to the industry. One of the best ways to accomplish said goals is to lead with an authentic and genuine desire to support the journey of our buyers to really build meaningful business relationships.

As it turns out, there's a lot more than meets the eye when it comes to authenticity. There's an enormous amount of research suggesting that being genuine is critical to overall sales performance. In fact, people that are genuine and have high emotional intelligence make more money annually than people that do not. Additionally, people that display these qualities tend to work better within a team, along with embracing change and knowing how to pivot to be successful.

Now, more than ever, authenticity is key in today's competitive sales landscape. Here are a few examples of genuine behavior while learning valuable techniques that will help you personally and professionally.

Passion: Many people simply pursue the path they believe will provide them with a steady income or big returns. Selecting a career based on these thought patterns is completely normal, but if it's the only factor that's considered, it can lead to an empty road ahead. Although the people that subscribe to this idea might find success, the fact of the matter is that the best salespeople are after much more than money.

Of course, the bottom line is still important to them, but it's not the be-all and end-all. On top of looking for a big paycheck, the top salesperson also wants to feel passionate about their work; tends to be mission-driven to stand by what their product or service does; and gets a magnificent sense of satisfaction when they help buyers win, which ultimately increases their chances of finding success. If you would like to amplify your passion for what you are doing on a daily basis, consider writing a few key things down daily—I promise that it makes a big difference. At the beginning of every day (it only takes a few minutes), think about and jot down what you are most grateful for, how you have grown in the week, and one new thing you can do or learn, or something that's keeping you up at night. For example, you could be grateful for a new chrome extension that helps you create efficiencies so that you can spend more time with your customers, or that you learned a new PowerPoint trick that went over really well.

You want to read a new sales productivity book by the end of the month, and you are trying to figure out the best way to get a particular big company's account, which you know has a need for your product/service, but they are not responding. Many people that decide to work in sales are high-achievers who have a knack for great conversation. They have a thirst for achieving their goals and everything that accompanies it, but sometimes they forget that hard work should also include humility.

Humble people tend to make the most effective leaders, and they are more likely to thrive and grow in solo and team dynamics. If this were not enough by itself, humble people are also more genuine and gracious when they interact with their customers and colleagues. They are the true magnets that all of us want to be around and emulate.

Just be genuine; people can spot a fake or a phony a mile away. Do the right things, and watch—well, you know—the magic!

Chapter 9

Getting You Started

Make Up Your Mind

This chapter of the book is aimed at helping you make some decisions. Here are some tips before making a decision about your spots: Create a constructive environment, investigate the situation in detail, generate good alternatives, explore your options, select your plan, communicate your decisions, and take action (make up your mind). Select the best solution once you have evaluated the alternatives, The next step is to make your decision. If one particular alternative is clearly better than the rest, your choice will be obvious. However, if you still have several competing options, there are plenty of tools that will help you decide between them.

If you have various criteria to consider, compare their reliability; or if you want to determine their relative importance, conduct a paired comparison analysis to decide which one should carry the most weight in your decision. You don't want to complicate the decision process, but you want to make the best decision. Remember, you have already done your research, so your top two or three should all be a good decision, but you still want the best of the top three.

Life is full of choices. Some are easy, such as what to have for dinner, and others are more serious, like for instance, choosing a career. Regardless of how important a decision is, good decision skills are useful in life, especially if you feel indecisive about something, and it's getting you down. Get tips on how to make good decisions, and find out what to do when you can't figure out a plan.

People make decisions throughout their day, most of which are straightforward and don't require much thought. However, when situations are more complicated and have longer-term impacts, it's easy to feel unsure or hesitant. When faced with tough decisions, it's common to feel overwhelmed, stressed, anxious, wound up, pressured, confused, distracted, and tired. Because indecision can have a negative impact on how you are feeling, it's important to learn strategies for making positive decisions in tough situations. While you may not be able to guarantee the outcome of a decision before you make it, at least you can know that you put a lot of careful thought into it.

Here are some tips for making decisions:

1. Don't let stress get the best of you. It's easy to feel stressed out and anxious when you are facing a tough choice. You might tend to rush your decisions without thinking them through, or you avoid making a decision at all because the stress has put you off your game. If you are feeling anxious about a decision, try to manage your stress so that it doesn't cloud your thinking. Go for a walk, hit up a workout, or hang out with some friends.

2. Give yourself some time. It's hard to think clearly under pressure, and sometimes your first idea is not always your best one. Give yourself the chance to sit on a problem for a while so that you can process your options and feel confident about the course of action you choose.

3. Weigh the pros and cons. When faced with big decisions, sometimes we lose sight of the big picture. Write a list of pros and cons for each course of action, and then compare them. Sometimes the cons are not as bad as we imagine them to be, or

the pros might make your options more obvious.

4. Think about your goals and values. It's important to be true to ourselves and what we value in life. When you factor into a decision the things that are important to you, the best option might become obvious. At any rate, you are more likely to end up with an outcome that you are happy with.

5. Consider all the possibilities. Making a decision can result in several different outcomes, and not all of them may be obvious. When considering each option, don't just list the positives and negatives; write down any likely consequences.

6. Talk it out. It can be helpful to get another person's perspective on your issues, particularly if they have faced similar decisions in their own life. Now that you have done your research, make a decision!

Stay Away from the Folly

Wow, this is a good one. When you get to your spot, there could be all kinds of people. Sometimes they are all good people, and sometimes you might have some bad people. However, you have done your research, and you have found the best place. These are the things we hate to talk about at times. Let's start with jealousy. Yep, I said it. It doesn't matter how professional you are; there is some professional jealousy out there, and you will run into some foolishness. I was working with a guy who was a bottom feeder on the sales report: He had two old cars; he was in a bad relationship with a baby mama; he had some brushes with the law (in and out of jail); and he was still walking around saying that people were jealous of him. Now, that is not jealousy—that is somebody that is crazy. I also remember a co-worker that would steal customers from other salespeople, and when he got caught stealing, he would get mad at you and not speak to you, like you had done something to him. In situations like that, you know that the person has a mental problem. The management should take care of this and get rid of the problem. If management doesn't handle it, you should keep notes, because it will turn into a big problem. Some of them have not had training. They were just put in a position that they were not qualified for.

Let's talk about this professional jealousy and what to do about it. In today's modern workplace, it's not uncommon to feel a little out of place. With the help of our numerous app notifications, we are constantly reminded about the seemingly more fun and interesting jobs that other people possess. We see them always traveling for work, posting about their posh brunch meetings, and perpetually bombarding our feeds with annoying hashtags like, "I love my job." Meanwhile, we are subjected to the small but terrible tyrannies of our work. We fall into the trap of comparing ourselves to our peers, and falsely believe that all those years spent being exemplary employees were just a waste of time. We wallow in self-pity, and slowly but surely begin to resent the work we once loved.

Take more responsibilities. It's not always the amount of money (or lack of) that causes jealousy in the workplace. It's actually the feeling of pointlessness—the belief that there's no more room for growth, and that you are better off being somewhere else, doing something else. It could be that a person stayed in their job for too long, or maybe they have outgrown the company. A lot of the times, however, it's simply because they have become weary of doing the same things day in and day out. To prevent the work from getting tedious, and from comparing yourself to what others have, challenge yourself to take on more responsibilities.

One of the things that most people feel jealous about are other people's success, or to be more exact, the speed at which they achieve their success. Say, for example, you and your friend both started out as managers, but for some reason, they landed a promotion and began earning more than you.

Before complaining about how the world is totally unfair, stop and think about the other factors that may have led to their promotion. Maybe there was a sudden vacancy, and they had the most experience. Maybe they spent longer hours in the office and were rewarded for it. Whatever the case may be, the best way to know about how people succeed is to ask them about it.

I hope this will help you. I don't want you to be the guy that has nothing going for him but is still thinking that someone is jealous of him. Keep a level head. If you take care of yourself and stay in your lane, everything will be fine. Pay no attention to people like the one I worked with. That is the way you deal with mental people on the job. Just stay focused, and you will stay on course! Stay away from the foolishness!

They Can Do It Without You

I have had so many friends that have been at a place for so long that they act as if the place can't run without them. When you find your spot, and you become really good (if you are reading this book, I know you will be awesome), keep a level head. At this point of your career, you will have to look out for this. You become so good that it's hard for someone to tell you anything. You will never know it all. There is always room for improvement. Never, never think that you know it all. Always look for ways to get better.

There is an old Italian word, *prima donna*. It has two meanings, but here is the one I am talking about. Prima donna: a very temperamental person with an inflated view of their own talent or importance. A prima donna type of person is an unpredictable person and a self-important person. You don't want to become this person. A prima donna is someone who acts like they are the star of the show. If you tirelessly dominate the conversation, and always interrupt when other people are talking, people will think that you are a prima donna. Remember not to become this person; but how do you deal with this person at the workplace? Focus on the content of their ideas, not their delivery style. If you don't have to deal with them, leave them alone. Stroke their ego, if you have to deal with them. Most managers will get rid of them.

I have always loved what I do as a professional salesperson, but I find it hard dealing with prima donnas. While difficult egos exist in every field, people whose livelihood is either based on their own personal brand or the brand of another individual, seem to find their way into the land of ridiculousness far quicker.

The way we treat others, and the words we use, have amazing power over both the lives of those we touch and our own. I know we can all look at others and wonder why they have to be so difficult. At the end of the day, however, the only people I can ensure to stop being so difficult is me. In doing that, perhaps I can help others along the path of life that models the phrase, "Just stay in your lane." Prima donnas, to put it quite simply, need their space. By allowing this person room to think not only about the business but about themselves, without guidance, can help them to realize they are troublesome.

There are some very simple ways to do this. Whether it's giving the prima donna an assignment that requires them to spend considerable time out of the office or away from other team members, you typically do not have to worry about their work ethic; and by isolating them, it ensures that they will not cause issues for other employees on this project. If the prima donna is a bad employee, this is also a great way to figure that out. If other team members made them look better than they were actually performing in the past, then that would no longer be an option. As a manager, it's a great way to learn more about this person as they work independently. In this book, you will learn not to be a prima donna, and will learn how to deal with one, as a manager or co-worker. They are the employee who thinks the rules don't apply to them, or that they are so valuable they should not have to follow the rules. They question everything, looking for loopholes, and generally make everyone a little crazy. The dictionary definition of this employee is "a vain or undisciplined person who finds it difficult to work under direction or part of a team." Dealing with this person is tough, but as we know, we must hold them accountable for the good of the team.

Have you ever heard the saying, "It ain't over until the 'fat lady' sings?" There is another dictionary definition of prima donna that's more complicated: "a principal female singer in an opera or concert organization." This prima donna is the lead. She's the fat lady that must sing before the opera can end. She can be the toughest person to deal with, because she honestly brings so much value to the organization. I think you get the picture: "They can't do it without you because you sell the most, and they will not get rid of you." Don't be surprised when they do. Just don't become a prima donna!

You Are There to Sell

I have seen so many people come to a sales team and think it's a social club. It is not a social club; you are there to sell. The sales industry has all kinds of fancy names: sales consultant, sales professional... and those names are fine, but remember that you are a salesperson, and you are there to sell. You are there to make sales results. A sales consultant is an experienced sales professional who uses their knowledge and skills to help businesses improve internal processes, and increase sales. They might work on behalf of a company or for themselves.

It's best to think of a sales professional as the bridge between your company and its customers. Remember, you have to sell yourself. Just as the best athletes constantly practice, improve, and refine their strategy, successful salespeople are always experimenting with existing techniques, and trying out new ones. After all, the second an athlete or rep stops striving to get better, they backslide.

I have collected one-sentence tips to keep you in peak selling shape. Whether you want to focus on your presentation skills, your approach to calling prospects, your methods for closing, or all of the above, you will find some great words of wisdom in this list.

Keeping up with your customers: It makes a customer feel good if you call them and wish them a happy birthday, and they will constantly send you referrals. When reaching out to a new or old customer, identify the problem that they need you to handle. Schedule time for prospecting each and every day, even on the last day of the month or quarter. Use multiple ways to prospect—email, phone, social media, events, referrals—keep your pipeline as full as possible. To get more responses, keep your emails simple so that anyone can read them. Keep your emails 10 words or less. You probably know that when you say you're just checking in, that doesn't work. Let it be something like a birthday, a child's birthday, a graduation, anniversary—anything— just let it be something. Once you get off the phone with someone, send a follow-up. Create activity; make it happen. Remember, you are there to sell!

I talked about something earlier in this book, called listening. You would not believe how many sales I have closed because of listening. Customers want your ear. When they feel that you are listening and that you can feel them, you are on your way to a close. Listening is probably the essential ingredient of being a success as a professional salesperson. The one attribute most often commented on about a well-liked salesperson is that he or she really listens. Salespeople who listen to their customers build rapport, swiftly clean up misunderstandings, increase respect, and build esteem in both themselves and others. Your communication style, which includes the way you listen, has a direct impact on the kind of environment you create around you. Please remember that statement.

Sometimes we put ourselves above the customer (we think we are better than they are). Wow... I know that is not you, but that's the signal you are sending. Keep your head up, do what you are trained to do, and watch the magic!

Chapter 10

Shoot for the Stars

Believe in a Power That's Greater Than You

I believe in Jesus. I am not telling you who your higher power should be; I am letting you know that I chose Jesus. I know that my higher power is working for me 24/7 in my lifetime. Life is bigger than you. I have met people where, after talking to them for a while, I get the impression that they think they are God. When times get a little hard, you will need this power to depend on. I'm telling you, there's nothing better than a higher power—in my case, it is Jesus. Love yourself; self-worth cannot be verified by others. You are worthy.

Nature and Revelations alike testify to God's love. Our God is the source of life, of wisdom, and of joy. Look at the wonderful and beautiful things of nature. Think of their marvelous adaptation to the needs and happiness of not only man but of all living creatures. The sunshine and the rain that refreshes the earth, hills, seas, and plains, all speak to us of the creator's love. It is God who supplies the daily needs of all His creatures. "The eyes of all wait upon thee; and thou givest them their meat in due season. Thou openest thine hand, and satisfied the desires of every living thing." (Psalm 145: 15–16)

I don't want to get religious here, but I wanted to let you know who my higher power is. When you know the greater power is with you, it keeps you positive and energized. I worked for a manager, and we had a super sales team. I called it the dream team. I believe we had the best team in Georgia. I know we were the best in the middle Georgia area. I am talking about a great team, and the manager screwed up the great team. He thought the company was doing well because of him. He thought that he was God, but he may have learned his lesson, because he is having a hard time finding good sales professionals.

Keep your feet on the ground when things are going well, and be thankful. Don't get a big head. *Higher power* is also a term that was used in the 1930s, in Alcoholics Anonymous, and is used in 12 other step programs. It is also sometimes referred to as a power greater than ourselves. The term sometimes refers to a Supreme Being, or deity or conceptions of God. Just know that believing in a higher power gives you that extra fuel you need to keep you getting to the next level.

Follow Your Goals and Plans

We talked about plans and goals earlier in this book. We are talking about it again because it is very important. Chances are that you have heard of the power of goal setting, and how people who set goals are 275% more likely to achieve significant results than those who simply don't set goals at all. You might know the different types of goals already, but you are still unsure of where to start. First things first, let's take a look at the term, *goals*. Goals are well-defined and focused. Here are 5 elements in setting goals. There are more, but these are the most important to me: specific, measurable, achievable, relevant, and time-based. A goal without a measureable outcome is like a sports competition without a scoreboard or scorekeeper. Effectively track your goals. To really achieve any goal that is worthwhile, discipline yourself to keep track until it's accomplished. Review your goals regularly, preferably every day. Break down a goal into actionable steps. Break down a goal into quantifiable results. Track a goal by the amount of time you spend on it.

When it comes to accomplishing goals, one thing that many people tend to neglect is that goals usually must be consistently tracked and reviewed. I want to point out the importance of tracking your goals, and suggest four different approaches for how to effectively track your goals. According to the nature of the goal itself, the main thing you can take away from this article is that no matter what type of goals you set, you should always find something to track your progress.

One of the main reasons that people don't get to accomplish their goals is that they tend to get distracted, and they lose track of important things that need to be done consistently in order to move forward toward their goals. Maybe you have set a perfectly achievable goal, and you have planned every detailed step but without effectively tracking your goal and knowing your progress. Most certainly, you will get discouraged when the first obstacle gets in the way, and you will end up giving up on your goal eventually. Keep yourself constantly reminded of your goals by reviewing them at a specific time each day. It could be in the morning, first thing after you get out of bed. It could be at night, just before you go to sleep. Write down all of your goals, or store them in computer software. When you review them, envision how accomplishing those goals will make you feel.

Check your current progress, understand what you did to move it forward, and find out what else you still need to do. By doing this regularly, you train your mind to become alert to things that are related to your goals, and gradually your mind will automatically guide you to do whatever is needed to achieve them. Make this your lifestyle. Stay on top of it. Like Mike says, "Just do it," and watch the magic!

Go Hard in the Paint

Let me explain what "in the paint" means. It's a basketball term; it's down in the painted area close to the goal, which is the high percentage spot. In other words, whatever you do, go at it hard. Don't be denied. Don't take "no" for an answer. We all have goals that we are striving to achieve. Setting goals is easy, but taking action to attain them can be difficult at times. But if you are passionate about it, you will surely find the way to get it done. However, there are times when you start to lose motivation. Don't get overwhelmed and decide to walk away. Instead, find your inspiration and motivation through the powerful words of wisdom (seek your higher power). Here are some quotes taken from different people across time and places in this world:

"If you want to live a happy life, tie it to a goal, not people or things." – Albert Einstein

"There is no substitute for hard work, 23 or 24 hours a day, and there is no substitute for patience and acceptance." – Caesar Chavez

"Plans are only good intentions unless they immediately degenerate into hard work." – Peter Drucker

"The road to success is not easy to navigate, but with hard work, drive, and passion, it's possible to achieve the American dream." – Tommy Hilfiger

"If you want to be happy, set goals that command your thoughts, liberate your energy, and inspire your hopes." – Andrew Carnegie

"Power means happiness; power means hard work and sacrifice." – Beyoncé Knowles

"I think that my biggest attribute to any success that I have had is hard work. There really is no substitute for working hard." – Maria Bartiromo

"All who have accomplished great things have had a great aim, have fixed their gaze on a goal that was high, one which sometimes seemed impossible." – Orison Swett Marden

"You have to set goals that are almost out of reach. If you set a goal that is attainable without much work or thought, you are stuck with something below your true talent and potential." – Steve Garvey

"A goal properly set is halfway reached." –Zig Ziglar

"If you set goals and go after them with all the determination you can muster, your gifts will take you places that will amaze you." – Les Brown

"Success is the progressive realization of a worthy goal or ideal." – Earl Nightingale

"You are always working to improve, and you are always being critiqued on your next performance. It's not about what you have done. There is always room to grow." – Misty Copeland.

"You can do anything if you set your goals. You just have to push yourself." – RJ Mitte

"Be practical as well as generous in your ideals. Keep your eyes on the stars but remember to keep your feet on the ground." – Theodore Roosevelt

"Impossible is just a word thrown around by small men who find it easier to live in the world they have been given than to explore the power they have to change it. Impossible is not a fact. It's an opinion. Impossible is potential. Impossible is temporary; impossible is nothing." – Muhammad Ali

"You are never too old to set goals or to dream a new dream." – C.S. Lewis

"Everybody wants to be famous, but nobody wants to do the work. I live by that. You grind hard so you can play harder. At the end of the

day, you put all the work in, and eventually it will pay off. It could be in a year; it could be in 30 years. Eventually, your hard work will pay off." – Keven Hart

"There are no secrets to success. It is the result of preparation, hard work, and learning from failure." – Colin Powell

"Things may come to those who wait but only the things left by those who hustle." – Abraham Lincoln

Those are some great quotes by great and successful people. Those are the ones I use when I need a little push. You can use them also, or you can get your own. Just keep yourself motivated and upbeat. You can make it happen; you will make it happen. Push hard, go hard in the paint, and watch the magic!

Save Some Money, Pay Ahead

This is another part of business that some people can't get right. I see them buy TVs, furniture, cars, and all types of stuff. It all gets repossessed at the end of the year. So when the selling is really good, put some of it away. That way, when it slows down, it won't be any pressure on you. When you put that kind of pressure on yourself, it makes it hard to perform at a peak (high peak) level. In professional selling, you want your mind to be at peace as much as possible, with no worries. I always say to get ahead on your bills. Start with it months ahead. Get as far ahead as you can but at least one month. I also recommend that you build a $1,000 emergency fund also. This would help you not get caught in those financial traps.

Learn how to live on a tight budget. You could be a single mother living paycheck to paycheck, or maybe you are a family who needs tips on living on a tight budget. Whatever your situation is, if you focus on it and have a plan, it makes the financial situation better. If you are living paycheck to paycheck, saving a full month's worth of income will alleviate the burden of waiting for each paycheck to come before determining your budget for the month. You would not have to wait for your paycheck to hit your account so that you could pay your bills. As a matter of fact, you would be putting yourself in a position to forget all about payday because, each month, you would create a budget based on the amount you earned last month. Essentially, you would be living on last month's income. Remember that simple changes can create big results.

Here are some more tips on debt, and there are also books and many resources out there. Everyone, with even a little bit of debt, has to manage their debt. If you just have a little debt, you have to keep up your payments and make sure it doesn't get out of control. On the other hand, when you have a large amount of debt, you have to put more effort into paying off your debt, while juggling payments on the debts you are not currently paying. Know who and how much you owe. Make a list of your debts, including the creditor, total amount of the debt, monthly payment, and due date. You can use your credit to confirm the debts on your list. Having all the debts in front of you will allow you to see the bigger picture and stay aware of your complete debt picture. Don't just create your list and forget about it. Refer to your debt list periodically, especially as you pay bills. Update your list every few months as the amount of your debts changes. Please pay your bills on time each month–late fees and other charges are more income leaving your home for no good reason. If you miss 2 payments in a row, your interest rate and finance charges will increase. I know that you know this stuff; this is just a reminder.

Create a monthly bill payment calendar. Use a bill payment calendar to help you figure out which bills to pay, with which paycheck. On your calendar, write each bill's payment amount next to that due date. Then fill in the date of each paycheck if you get paid on the same days every month, like the 1st and 15th. You can use the same calendar from month to month, but if your paycheck falls on different days of the month, it would help to create a new calendar for each month.

Whatever you do with your finances, create a budget. Find one that will work for you, I have seen so many really good sales professionals fail because of their finances. Don't let this happen to you; live below your means. It's hard trying to make a sale, knowing that someone is coming to get your car at the same time. Just keep this in mind as you go on your sales journey—it will make all the difference!

Don't Worry About Keeping up with the Joneses

Are you tired of keeping up with the Joneses? They don't want you to know that they are actually broke! This chapter kind of mixes in with the last chapter. I have seen lots of salespeople get in trouble trying to be like or keep up with other people. Living on less than you make is a matter of controlling yourself, not a matter of math. People who live below their means enjoy a freedom that people busy upgrading their lifestyles cannot fathom. Everything you spend needs a line in your budget, even gifts and other miscellaneous spending. Have a plan for it. I am in competition with no one. I have no desire to play the game of being better than anyone else. I am simply trying to be better than the person I was yesterday. No matter how big your house is, how recent your car is, or how big your bank account is, your grave will always be the same size as everyone else's. Stay humble. I know you have heard this before. Rich people stay rich by living like they're broke, and broke people stay broke by living like they're rich (that's so true). Stop trying to keep up with the Joneses. It's a dead-end road. Being in control of your finances is the best stress reliever. Make yourself rich by making yourself want less.

This is what the great Warren Buffet has to say about it: *"Never depend on one income." "If you buy things you don't need, soon you will sell things that you don't need." "Don't save what is left after spending, but spend what is left after saving." "Do not put all your eggs in one basket." "Honesty is a very expensive gift; do not expect it from cheap people."*

Just keep your finances under control. It will save you a lot of pain. Debt is the slavery of the free. Having a budget doesn't mean you can't have fun. It means you make a plan and don't let your expenses get out of control. Life is about balance. Be kind, but don't let people abuse you. Trust, but don't be deceived. Be content, but never stop improving yourself.

Long before Facebook and Instagram made us *insta-jealous*, folks were intimidated by their neighbors and keeping up with the Joneses. That was the term used to described being envious and influenced by what people in your circle had and were doing. Keeping up with other people causes debt and a sense of greed. That is no way to live. Comparing lifestyles and judging yours as inadequate will never help you make better decisions, because you simply don't know how the Joneses got what they have.

Don't worry about keeping up with the Joneses. Worry about staying in your lane, in your budget, and on track for your wealth. I could go on and on, but I think you get the picture. Don't let that kind of thinking happen to you. As I come to the close of writing this book, I want to thank you all for your support. I have lots of experience in the field of selling, and I hope this book will help you on your journey of selling. This is why I want to share it with you.

The pitfalls I had are in this book. I put them there so that you don't have them, which will give you a head start, if you use them. This book has been a great journey for me. It took longer than I planned, but I wanted to get everything out of me and put it in a book to help someone.

I have been to lots of workshops and seminars to listen to people who have never been on a sales floor, and to some that have had little time on the sales floor. I have been in sales for 35-plus years. I have been the infantry in the foxhole, and have seen so many sales situations.

Again, thank you. I look forward to seeing you on top of the leader's board in your company!

JUST WATCH THE MAGIC!!!

www.ingramcontent.com/pod-product-compliance
Lightning Source LLC
Chambersburg PA
CBHW071155200326
41519CB00018B/5232